MAURITANIA'S CAMPAIGN OF TERROR

State-Sponsored Repression of Black Africans

Human Rights Watch/Africa
(formerly Africa Watch)

Human Rights Watch
New York • Washington • Los Angeles • London

Printed in the United States of America.

Library of Congress Catalog Card Number: 94-75822
ISBN: 1-56432-133-9

Human Rights Watch/Africa (formerly Africa Watch)
Human Rights Watch/Africa is a non-governmental organization established in 1988 to monitor promote the observance of internationally recognized human rights in Africa. Abdullahi An-Na'im is the director; Janet Fleischman is the Washington representative; Karen Sorensen, Alex Vines, and Berhane Woldegabriel are research associates; Kimberly Mazyck and Urmi Shah are associates; Bronwen Manby is a consultant. William Carmichael is the chair of the advisory committee and Alice Brown is the vice-chair.

HUMAN RIGHTS WATCH

Human Rights Watch conducts regular, systematic investigations of human rights abuses in some seventy countries around the world. It addresses the human rights practices of governments of all political stripes, of all geopolitical alignments, and of all ethnic and religious persuasions. In internal wars it documents violations by both governments and rebel groups. Human Rights Watch defends freedom of thought and expression, due process and equal protection of the law; it documents and denounces murders, disappearances, torture, arbitrary imprisonment, exile, censorship and other abuses of internationally recognized human rights.

Human Rights Watch began in 1978 with the founding of its Helsinki division. Today, it includes five divisions covering Africa, the Americas, Asia, the Middle East, as well as the signatories of the Helsinki accords. It also includes four collaborative projects on arms, free expression, prison conditions, and women's rights. It maintains offices in New York, Washington, Los Angeles, London, Moscow, Belgrade, Zagreb and Hong Kong. Human Rights Watch is an independent, nongovernmental organization, supported by contributions from private individuals and foundations. It accepts no government funds, directly or indirectly.

The staff includes Kenneth Roth, executive director; Cynthia Brown, program director; Holly J. Burkhalter, advocacy director; Allyson Collins, research associate; Richard Dicker, associate counsel; Jamie Fellner, foundation relations director; Hamilton Fish, Jr., senior advisor; Barbara Guglielmo, comptroller; Robert Kimzey, publications director; Gara LaMarche, associate director; Michal Longfelder, development director; Ellen Lutz, California director; Juan Méndez, general counsel; Susan Osnos, communications director; Dinah PoKempner, research associate; Jemera Rone, counsel; Rachel Weintraub, special events director; and Derrick Wong, finance and administration director.

The regional directors of Human Rights Watch are Abdullahi An-Na'im, Africa; Juan E. Méndez, Americas; Sidney Jones, Asia; Jeri Laber, Helsinki; and Andrew Whitley, Middle East. The project directors are Kenneth Anderson, Arms Project; Gara LaMarche, Free Expression Project; Joanna Weschler, Prison Project; and Dorothy Q. Thomas, Women's Rights Project.

Addresses for Human Rights Watch

485 Fifth Avenue
New York, NY 10017-6104
Tel: (212) 972-8400
Fax: (212) 972-0905
email: hrwatchnyc@igc.apc.org

1522 K Street, N.W., #910
Washington, DC 20005
Tel: (202) 371-6592
Fax: (202) 371-0124
email: hrwatchdc@igc.apc.org

10951 West Pico Blvd., #203
Los Angeles, CA 90064
Tel: (310) 475-3070
Fax: (310) 475-5613
email: hrwatchla@igc.apc.org

90 Borough High Street
London, UK SE1 1LL
Tel: (071) 378-8008
Fax: (071) 378-8029
email: hrwatchuk@gn.apc.org

ACKNOWLEDGEMENTS

This report was written by Janet Fleischman, Washington representative of Human Rights Watch/Africa. It is based on three fact-finding missions to Senegal -- in May-June 1990, February-March 1991, and October-November 1993 -- as well as numerous interviews conducted in Paris, New York, and Washington.

Human Rights Watch/Africa gratefully acknowledges the following staff members who assisted with editing and producing this report: Abdullahi An-Na'im; Karen Sorensen; and Kim Mazyck. In addition, we would like to thank Rakiya Omaar and Alex de Waal for their contributions. Most importantly, we express our sincere thanks to the many Mauritanians, most of whom must remain nameless for their own protection and that of their families, who provided invaluable assistance throughout this project.

TABLE OF CONTENTS

1
INTRODUCTION AND SUMMARY OF FINDINGS

Long before "ethnic cleansing" entered popular parlance, its effects were painfully apparent in Mauritania. Since 1989, tens of thousands of black Mauritanians have been forcibly expelled, and hundreds more have been tortured or killed; an undeclared military occupation of the Senegal River Valley, where many of the blacks live, subjects those who remained to harsh repression. The campaign to eliminate black culture in Mauritania, orchestrated by the white Moor rulers, reached its height in the late 1980s and early 1990s, and continues today.

The Mauritanian authorities flatly deny these human rights violations, and they continue to block efforts to seek accountability for past abuses. Part of the government's strategy has been to deny access to Mauritania by international observers; Human Rights Watch/Africa, for example, has been denied permission to conduct a human rights investigation in Mauritania, despite repeated requests since the fall of 1989.[1]

Mauritania is ripe for government manipulation of ethnic conflict. Straddling the seam between the Arab world and black Africa, the population has been ruled by the *beydanes* -- literally "white men" of Arab-Berber descent, also known as Moors -- who have subjected the black population to gross violations of human rights. The black population is divided into two categories: the black ethnic groups of Halpulaar, Soninké, Wolof, and Bambara; and the *haratines*, also known as black Moors, who are former black slaves who remain politically and culturally tied to their former masters. The Halpulaar, which is the largest black ethnic group, has been considered by the government to constitute the most serious opposition. Each group -- the beydanes, the haratines, and the blacks -- constitutes about one third of the population, although that information is so threatening that the government refuses to release census figures.

---

[1]In January 1994, the Mauritanian government permitted a delegation representing Agir Ensemble Pour Les Droits de l'Homme, a French human rights group, and the Paris-based International Federation for Human Rights (FIDH), to visit the country. However, soon after the delegation left Mauritania, the vice president of the Mauritanian Human Rights Association (AMDH), Professor Cheikh Saad Bouh Kamara, was arrested for four days without charge, apparently in connection with the human rights mission. His detention exerts a chilling effect on international organizations that seek to conduct independent human rights investigations in Mauritania.

The abuses against blacks in Mauritania date back to the early years of independence, but have been especially acute since the 1980s. Tension between the beydanes, who effectively controlled the country, and the blacks, who held most mid-level government jobs, increased in the 1960s and 1970s. The black population's fears of Arab domination were accentuated as the Mauritanian authorities pursued policies designed to favor Arab culture and Arabic speakers - particularly the beydanes, but also haratines -- to the detriment of the black African population. Although the blacks and the Moors are all Muslim, the blacks resented Islam being equated with Arabism, and sought to preserve their own culture and heritage. Arabization was used to marginalize the black populations, and has penetrated most aspects of Mauritanian life: the educational system; the language, with Arabic replacing French as the official language; the administration of justice, in both regular and religious courts; employment practices; access to loans and credits; and so forth.

In December 1984, while President Haidalla was out of the country, Lt.Col. Maaouiya Ould Sid'Ahmed Taya seized power in a bloodless coup and became President. During his rule, which continues today, the persecution of the black ethnic groups escalated.

Black opposition to the government's policies grew in the mid-1980s, some elements of which coalesced around a clandestine organization of black intellectuals called the African Liberation Forces of Mauritania (FLAM). In 1986, FLAM issued "The Manifesto of the Oppressed Black Mauritanian," which detailed the domination of Mauritanian society by the beydanes and the persecution of the blacks. The government responded by arresting twenty-one of the FLAM leaders, subjecting them to torture and long prison terms. The crackdown on FLAM signalled an intensification of the government's battle against the blacks.

Despite this history of persecution, no one was prepared for two governmental campaigns that followed. In April 1989, a border dispute between Mauritania and Senegal erupted into ethnic violence, led to the deportation of thousands of both countries' nationals, and brought the two countries to the brink of war. The Mauritanian government used the dispute to begin expelling thousands of blacks from Mauritania, accusing them of being Senegalese. The expulsions were accompanied by extrajudicial executions, torture, and the confiscation of property. As of late 1993, United Nations estimates put the number of Mauritanian refugees in Senegal at approximately 52,500, and in Mali at some 13,000. The real figures are probably substantially higher, since this number reflects only those who have formally registered with the local authorities, and does not take into account the thousands living with relatives on the Senegalese side of the river.

The government's campaign against blacks escalated between late 1990 and early 1991, with the massacre of over 500 blacks in the military and the civil service. The victims were among the approximately 3,000 blacks who were arrested without charge, held in incommunicado detention, and subjected to vicious physical abuse, allegedly for planning a coup. Although high-ranking government officials orchestrated the massacre, the government refuses to acknowledge responsibility for the deaths or to permit an independent investigation.

There is another critical factor in the government's campaign against the blacks -- the land along the Senegal River Valley, which had belonged to the local black populations for generations. By the mid-1980s, black lands were being expropriated by the authorities and given to beydane businessmen, a process that was accelerated with the expulsions. The conflict over land has led to widespread human rights abuses against the blacks, and has drastically altered the economic and social character of the Senegal River Valley.

After Mauritania sided with Iraq in the Gulf War, it lost the economic support of the Gulf states and much of the West other than France, and was desperate to rebuild its international credibility. Accordingly, in April 1991 the government announced that it was embarking on the path of democratization; presidential elections were held in January 1992 but were marred by serious irregularities and fraud. The regime clearly hoped to regain foreign aid and to conceal responsibility for human rights abuses.

Despite cosmetic democratization and a lessening of government-instigated violence since 1992, Mauritania retains all the apparatus of a repressive state with a disregard for basic human rights. The new, civilian government, which is virtually identical to its military predecessor, continues to be responsible for human rights abuses. An undeclared state of emergency continues along the Senegal River Valley, characterized by a chronic and insidious pattern of violations against blacks, including indiscriminate killings, detention, rape, and beatings by the security forces. The government no longer needs to resort to large-scale expulsions and killings; it is now institutionalizing its control over the black population.

In a positive development, the new government has become more tolerant of criticism from the opposition. An independent press has been able to operate since late 1991, and numerous articles have been published that are critical of the government and its human rights policies. However, the government still controls radio and television, and given the high rate of illiteracy in Mauritania, the broadcast media remain the primary source of information.

In addition, some human rights activities have been permitted, including occasional meetings, demonstrations, and investigations. Yet the authorities refuse to recognize the leading independent human rights organization, the Mauritanian Human Rights Association (AMDH), despite its repeated requests over the past two years. The government does recognize the Mauritanian League for Human Rights, which usually supports the government.

THE NEED FOR ACCOUNTABILITY

Despite abundant evidence directly linking high-ranking government officials to human rights abuses against the black ethnic groups, the Mauritanian government refuses to acknowledge responsibility or to allow any independent investigation. In order to guarantee immunity for those responsible and to block any attempts at accountability for past abuses, an amnesty was declared in June 1993 covering all crimes committed by the armed forces and security forces between April 1989 and April 1992. It is no coincidence that this period corresponds to the height of the abuses against Mauritania's blacks, especially the massacre of 500-600 black Africans in 1990-91. Human Rights Watch/Africa believes that those responsible for egregious human rights abuses in Mauritania must be held accountable for their crimes; it is the responsibility of governments to seek accountability, regardless of whether the perpetrators are officials of the government, the military, anti-government forces, or others. Human Rights Watch/Africa opposes any laws that purport to immunize those who have committed gross abuses from exposure of their crime, from civil suits for damages for those crimes, or from criminal investigation, prosecution and punishment.

The obligation to investigate gross abuses of human rights is clearly spelled out in international law, which is widely accepted as having created a duty to investigate and punish abuses of rights. Examples of such a standard are included in the U.N. Convention Against Torture and Other Forms of Cruel, Inhuman or Degrading Treatment or Punishment, which specifically establishes the duty to bring torturers to justice, and the Universal Declaration of Human Rights, which requires states to provide an effective remedy for abuses. The combination of all such provisions is widely accepted as having created a duty to investigate and punish gross abuses of huan rights. Mauritania is also bound by the international treaties that is has ratified, including the Slavery Convention of 1926.

Mauritanian refugees also demand that those responsible for human rights violations against the blacks be brought to justice. "What happened [in Mauritania] can't ever happen again," a refugee from Selibaby explained.

"There has to be a total change. But under these conditions, I can't go back."[2] The same point was made even more strongly by a widow of one of the soldiers killed in the 1991 massacre. "The material things are secondary," she said. "What matters most is justice."[3]

SUMMARY OF FINDINGS

- In 1989–1990, tens of thousands of black Africans were forcibly expelled from Mauritania. The expulsions were accompanied by extrajudicial executions, arbitrary arrests, torture, rape, theft of property, and destruction of legal documents. Those targeted included professionals in the cities, landholders along the Senegal River Valley, and nomadic herders. Though mass expulsions ended in 1990, the military continued to expel smaller numbers of black Mauritanians, and blacks still flee in search of refuge in Senegal or Mali.
- A principal focus of the conflict between the beydanes and the blacks has been the land along the Senegal River Valley. Successive Mauritanian governments have tried to take over control of the land, a policy that has led to widespread human rights abuses against the blacks, characterized by state-sponsored violence and a complete lack of due process.
- From November 1990 through February 1991, 500–600 black political prisoners were executed or tortured to death by government forces. The victims were among the approximately 2,500 blacks arrested without charge, held in incommunicado detention, and subjected to vicious physical abuse.
- Slavery continues to exist in Mauritania, especially in the countryside. Its persistence is due to inadequate efforts by the government to educate slaves about their rights and to prosecute slaveholders for continuing to own slaves. Those slaves who attempt to escape are sometimes subjected to severe punishment and torture.
- Black Africans in Mauritania are subjected to *de facto* discriminatory government policies, such as forced Arabization, with serious consequences for their civil and political rights. The discriminatory

---

[2]Interview in Bakel, Senegal, October 28, 1993.

[3]Interview in Ourosogui, Department of Matam, Senegal, October 30, 1993.

effects of Arabization are apparent in the suppression of the black communities' freedom of expression and association.

- A pattern of human rights violations continues today against black Mauritanians in the Senegal River Valley, including indiscriminate killing, detention, torture, rape, and beatings by the military and security forces. No semblance of the rule of law exists. While the rate of killings diminished since 1992, the remaining black populations face great difficulties obtaining official identity documents, employment, bank loans, and land.
- Mauritanian authorities have refused to investigate, prosecute, or punish those responsible for such gross abuses as the deportations and the massacre of prisoners, despite ample evidence pointing to the direct involvement of many high-ranking government officials.
- The independent press has become a more vibrant force since 1992. Independent journalists investigated and wrote about government abuses, both past and present, but the government still controls radio and television.

2
BACKGROUND[1]

The Islamic Republic of Mauritania, a desert country of approximately two million people on the West African coast, forms a geographical bridge between Arab North Africa and black sub-Saharan Africa. The country is an artificial creation linking the largely nomadic Arab-Berber north with the sedentary black African south. Since independence from France in November 1960, the country has been ruled by the *beydanes* -- literally "white men" of Arab-Berber descent, also known as Moors -- who have subjected the black ethnic groups to gross violations of human rights.

The black population is divided into two categories: the black ethnic groups of Halpulaar, Soninké, Wolof, and Bambara; and the *haratines*, also known as black Moors, who are former black slaves who remain politically and culturally tied to their former masters.[2] The Halpulaar, which is the largest black ethnic group, has been considered by the government to constitute the most serious opposition. The population statistics are a matter of debate because the government has refused to publish the results of the 1988 census. The government claims that the population is 70 percent Moor, though many blacks contend that they represent as much as two-thirds of the population, including the black Moors.

Mauritania became a French colony in 1920. During the colonial period, the French administered Mauritania indirectly, through the existing Moor structures. After World War II, France was constrained to permit reform or independence for its colonies, Mauritania included, although there was not a great deal of pro-independence activity in the country. Mauritania was divided on the question of independence: Many of the Moors supported a union with Morocco, and many of the blacks favored a merger with Senegal and Mali.

---

[1]Background sources include: Francis de Chassey, *Mauritanie 1900-1975*. Paris: Editions l'Harmattan, 1985; Robert E. Handloff, Editor, *Mauritania: A Country Study*. Washington: Federal Research Division of the Library of Congress, 1990; "Mauritania," *Africa South of the Sahara*; "Mauritania," *EIU Country Profile*.

[2]Not all haratines have kept these ties to their former masters. In 1974, a group of haratine intellectuals formed a movement called El Hor (The Free). El Hor fought for an end to slavery in Mauritania and grew into a significant political force. See the chapter on Slavery.

Nevertheless, the country became independent on November 28, 1960, under the presidency of Moktar Ould Daddah, who quickly abandoned the multi-party system and instituted one-party rule.

Since Morocco claimed part of Mauritania's territory, most of the Arab countries refused to recognize Mauritania officially during the first few years of independence.[3] Accordingly, throughout most of the 1960s, Mauritania relied heavily on France for diplomatic and economic support. Extensive agreements were signed between the two countries covering military, economic, cultural, and technical cooperation. In return, France occupied a privileged position regarding ties to the Mauritanian administration and use of Mauritanian territory -- air, sea, and land.

The early years of independence were difficult. Tension between the Moors, who effectively controlled the country, and the blacks, who held most mid-level government jobs, increased. The black population's fears of Arab domination were accentuated as the government introduced measures designed to "Arabize" the country, notably the decision in 1966 to require all students to study Arabic. The linguistic and educational questions became points of serious contention between the black and Moor communities, with the black groups preferring to study and speak in French as a means of resisting Arabization and retaining links with francophone black Africa. Although the blacks and the Moors are all Muslim, the blacks resented Islam being equated with Arabism, and sought to preserve their own culture and heritage.

The economic problems were aggravated in the late 1960s and early 1970s by a severe drought, which contributed to a massive movement of the nomadic population into urban areas. This demographic shift had profound ramifications throughout the country: in 1965, an estimated 83 percent of Mauritania's population led a nomadic or semi-nomadic life; by 1987, only 23 percent were nomadic.[4] In addition, the drought drove many of the remaining nomads toward the fertile Senegal , an area occupied largely by the black ethnic groups. The land along the valley soon took on new economic importance for the country.

In the early 1970s, the government's political and economic policies became more independent and nationalistic. By enlisting other countries to provide financial support -- including Iraq, Egypt, Kuwait, Libya, and China --

---

[3]Morocco did not recognize Mauritania until 1969.

[4]"Mauritania: Summary Report," Economic Intelligence Unit Country Profile 1989-90.

Mauritania began to distance itself from France's influence. In 1972, Mauritania was one of the first countries of francophone Africa to announce that it would review its cooperation agreements with France, which had been signed at independence. The following year, Mauritania signed new, less sweeping agreements with France, which still included cultural, technical, and economic cooperation, but excluded military and monetary agreements. It also decided to leave the franc zone[5] and create a new national currency -- the *ouguiya*.

Other signs of this increasing nationalism were soon apparent, including Mauritania's decision to join the Arab League in 1973. In 1974, the decision was made to nationalize the Mauritanian Iron Mines Company (MIFERMA), which, although it dominated the economy, was controlled by French interests.[6] In its desire to be a more integral part of the Arab world, Mauritania also began to send students (usually Moors) for education and training in countries like Iraq, Syria, and Saudi Arabia. Upon their return, these students pursued strategies for further Arabization.

In 1975, Mauritania began its costly involvement in the war in the Western Sahara, formerly known as the Spanish Sahara, which was about to be decolonized from Spain. In October 1975, the International Court of Justice in the Hague ruled that neither Morocco nor Mauritania had a right to sovereignty over Western Sahara, and that the people had a right to self-determination. However, in November 1975, Spain, Morocco, and Mauritania signed the Madrid Agreement, which provided for the area to be divided between Morocco and Mauritania. Fierce opposition to the agreement resulted in the formation of a guerrilla group known as the Polisario Front, an acronym for the Popular Front for the Liberation of Saguia el Hamra and Rio de Oro. The group, backed by Algeria, declared the area independent and renamed it the Sahrawi Arab Democratic Republic (SADR), backed by Algeria.

The war forced Mauritania to expand greatly its armed forces -- from some 3,000 in 1976 to 15,000–17,000 in 1978 -- thus burdening an already weak economy. This military build-up, which was financed with the aid of countries such as Saudi Arabia, served to strengthen the power of the military within society. In order to satisfy the demand for soldiers, blacks were recruited in

---

[5]The franc zone is a group of fourteen African countries whose currencies are based on the French franc.

[6]MIFERMA was responsible for some eighty percent of the country's exports. After it was nationalized, the company's name was changed to National Mining and Industrial Company (SNIM).

large numbers to fight the Polisario guerrillas, even though they opposed annexing the territory because it would increase the threat of Arab domination. Many Moors also opposed the war, because of their cultural and familial ties to the Polisario and the people of the Western Sahara.

In July 1978, with the economy in ruins and no prospect for a Mauritanian victory, Col. Mustapha Ould Salek and other military officers launched a coup and established a ruling Military Committee for National Recovery (CMRN). Less than a year later, in April 1979, Col. Ahmed Ould Bouceif and Col. Mohamed Khouna Ould Haidalla overthrew Salek's government. In May, Colonel Bouceif died in an airplane crash, and Haidalla became prime minister with Col. Mohamed Louly as president; in January 1980, Haidalla became president of the Military Committee for National Salvation (CMSN). As soon as Haidalla became president, he announced that Mauritania would adopt a policy of neutrality in the Western Sahara conflict. He also abolished slavery, although no serious steps were taken to implement the decision. By the end of 1980, a civilian government was formed, and progress was made toward establishing a democratic, multiparty government. However, these efforts were abandoned in April 1981, after a failed coup attempt in March by pro-Moroccan forces; the coup leaders were executed. A month later, Haidalla and the CMSN transformed the civilian government into a military one, with Lt.Col. Maaouiya Ould Sid'Ahmed Taya as chief of staff.

In December 1984, while Haidalla was attending a Franco-African summit in Burundi, Colonel Taya seized power in a bloodless coup and became president. During his rule, which continues today, the persecution of the black ethnic groups escalated. The Baathist and Nasserite[7] movements also gained strength. This set the stage for the acute repression against the black ethnic groups in the late 1980s and early 1990s.

---

[7]The Baathists are radical, pan-Arab nationalists associated with the ruling parties of Iraq and Syria. The Nasserites are committed to the Arab, nationalist ideology of Jamal Abdel Nasser of Egypt.

3
FORCIBLE EXPULSIONS

On April 9, 1989, in Diawara, a village on an island in the Senegal River, a conflict between Mauritanian herders and Senegalese farmers resulted in the killing of two Senegalese. This incident -- for which Senegal held Mauritanian authorities responsible, although Mauritania repeatedly denied it -- sparked a chain of events that brought Senegal and Mauritania to the brink of war. The hostility between the two countries provoked an eruption of ethnic violence and killing that rapidly led to the expulsion of tens of thousands of blacks from Mauritania, accompanied by widespread extrajudicial executions, arbitrary arrests, torture, rape, and confiscation of property.

One of the factors underlying the conflict with Senegal and the expulsions of the blacks was the tendency of the beydanes to see black Mauritanians as synonymous with Senegalese; Mauritanian citizenship itself counted for less than racial identity. Therefore, the beydanes saw a logic in taking reprisals against black Mauritanians in response to attacks on white Mauritanians by Senegalese.

There is no evidence indicating that the expulsions were part of a premeditated "grand plan" by the Mauritanian authorities to eliminate its black population. Rather, it seems that the authorities were taking advantage of an opportunity not only to further their efforts to "arabize" the country, but also to retaliate against the black ethnic groups for the attacks against Mauritanian Moors in Senegal. Clearly, the expulsions were also an effort to terrorize the black population.

The expulsions should be viewed in the context of the traditional structure of society along the river valley. For hundreds of years, the river had been an artery of communication and trade; the center of society, the antithesis of a frontier. The river used to be, as one Mauritanian explained, "like a street in the village": families frequently lived and farmed on both sides of the river; traffic in the form of *pirogues* or canoes and commerce flowed freely back and forth. The notion of the river as an administrative and political border was wholly contrary to local customs and traditions.

During the colonial period, the territory comprising what is now Senegal and Mauritania was governed from St. Louis in Senegal. Despite the creation of two separate countries in 1960,[1] life along the river valley was relatively

---

[1]The border between the two former French colonies was established by decree in December 1933.

unchanged for much of the population. Local residents had little need for official papers, such as identity cards, except if they intended to pursue higher education or special employment; therefore, most blacks in the valley had no papers identifying their nationality. Many blacks studied in St. Louis or Dakar, where there were institutions of higher education, or travelled to the cities in search of employment, but returned later to live in Mauritania. In addition, the Peul herders, whose nomadic life was based on unrestricted movement, considered the pastures on both sides of the river to be their natural preserve.

The fact that the colonial administrative capital, St Louis, was placed in Senegal at the time of independence meant that Mauritanian civil servants of the colonial era lived and worked in what became Senegal; their children were born there. Those who later moved to Nouakchott or retired to Mauritania, and especially their children, were vulnerable in 1989 to the charge of originating from Senegal, and many were expelled.

Given the mobility of the population in this region, the events of 1989-90 came as an acute shock to the local population. Suddenly, the Mauritanian side of the river was transformed into a military zone, with guards stationed throughout and a curfew imposed. The effect was that of an undeclared state of emergency. The river itself became a "no man's land," which local residents no longer dared to enter. Families and villages were split apart, and communication became almost impossible.

Although the massive expulsions ended in 1990, isolated instances of expulsions, arrests, and killings continued until and throughout 1993. The Senegal River Valley is under a form of military occupation, with numerous military bases ensuring that an atmosphere of general repression remains.

THE RIOTS IN DAKAR AND NOUAKCHOTT

Following the border clashes in Diawara which left two Senegalese dead, violent anti-Mauritanian riots erupted in Bakel, Dakar, and other towns in Senegal. The retail trade in Senegal was dominated by Mauritanians, and many of their shops were pillaged. Mark Doyle, a British journalist who was based in Dakar, wrote the following account of the mayhem there:

> Almost as soon as the news was out that two Senegalese had been killed at a remote spot on the border -- shot, according to the Senegalese media, by Mauritanians -- the looting of Mauritanian-owned shops began in the nearest town, Bakel. Senegalese police had to take Mauritanians under their protection to stop angry villagers from attacking them. This scenario was to be repeated throughout

> Senegal....[i]n the outskirts of [Dakar], the systematic pillaging of Mauritanian-owned shops seemed to have become a national sport.[2]

On April 22 and 23, the attacks on Mauritanian boutiques in Dakar began in earnest. Much of the destruction was reportedly carried out by roving bands of unemployed young people. The fact that the unemployed youths were responsible for much of the destruction and violence has led many observers to link the events in Dakar with rising frustration concerning the economic and political situation in Senegal. Police in Dakar finally restored order on Sunday night, April 23.

The events in Dakar sparked anti-Senegalese riots in Nouakchott. On Monday, April 24, the tension increased in Nouakchott and Nouadhibou as news spread about the pillaging in Senegal, and a campaign of terror was unleashed against black Mauritanians on April 24 and 25. Late Monday and into Tuesday, armed haratines were trucked into Senegalese areas of the cities.[3] Black Mauritanians, Senegalese, and other black Africans were viciously attacked, subjected to a range of atrocities, and often clubbed to death. Although no precise figures are available, it is believed that at least 150-200 blacks were killed. On Tuesday, April 25, the Mauritanian government declared a curfew in Nouakchott and Nouadhibou.

A foreign relief worker who was in Nouakchott at the time of the rioting described the brutality he witnessed as follows:

> A mob came up the street and, at the intersection, came upon a house, no different from others in the area, but thought to be Senegalese. The youths started throwing rocks and sticks over the wall at the house, glass started breaking, then they got in the door. It was so sad to watch from [where I was], helpless. Several minutes passed while many more people came and joined the crowd trying to get through the doorway like a swarm. Then they started coming out with books, then throwing them up in the air and ripping out the pages; two guys were dragging a refrigerator; several had chairs and beds on their heads, starting to run down the street. Passing traffic

---

[2]Mark Doyle, "Blood Brothers," *Africa Report*, (New York), July-August 1989, p. 14.

[3]According to some reports, they brought with them lists of names of Senegalese living there, which may have come from a census taken several months before.

> slowed, watched, then continued....The house...was owned by a black Mauritanian whose last name happened to be Senghor, like the first president of Senegal. He's a Mauritanian diplomat of all things.[4]

He reported that the black population remained terrified days after the rampaging in Nouakchott.

> The horror of the night two days ago was still evident in the scared and unsure faces of everyone on the streets. What began as retaliation against Senegalese ended up being a massacre of anyone who was a black African. Senegalese formed the majority of the deaths, but Malians, Guineans, and Mauritanians -- Pulaars, Wolofs, and Soninkés -- were also among the toll. Ironically, the main force of the mobs were the black Moors, who struck with such a vengeance -- beating, killing, and robbing black Africans. It just turned into a free for all. First picking out Senegalese shops, then their persons, then all black-owned shops and homes, and then eventually lives....At the hospital are piles of bodies, unclaimed. The authorities aren't letting people identify bodies. There are many in Nouakchott who have no idea if their relatives or friends are dead, injured, or alive.
>
> All black African businesses are history. All the tailors had their machines smashed, or stolen. The cloth sellers were beaten, stores smashed and cloth stolen. Music stores were ransacked and smashed. All the photography studios in town were black African-owned and had their equipment stolen. Most of the local restaurants were black African-owned and had their refrigerators stolen, tables smashed, pots, pans, and utensils stolen.

At first, the magnitude of the killings in Nouakchott was not known in Senegal. Government sources and press reports indicated that some twenty persons had died, though the actual figures were many times that number. By the week's end, when the picture became clearer, violence again exploded in Senegalese cities, including Dakar. Doyle wrote:

---

[4]Anonymous letter from Nouakchott, Mauritania, April 1989.

> In revenge for the killings in Mauritania, the mob cornered mostly white Moors who had not yet taken refuge and brutally murdered them. Most of the killing was in Dakar. I personally counted 38 bodies of Mauritanians in the central mortuary, including the bodies of two tiny infants whose heads had been smashed in. While at least 38 Moors were killed in Dakar, police sources said 12 had been killed in the central Senegalese town of Touba and four were killed in nearby Djiorbel. When other incidents were added, the final tally appeared to be between 50 and 60, but again the figure could not be definitive.[5]

Under intense international pressure to prevent further bloodshed, Senegal and Mauritania agreed to repatriate each others' citizens. An international airlift was organized, and France, Spain, Algeria, and Morocco provided airplanes to facilitate the repatriation program. An estimated 100,000 Mauritanians and 85,000 Senegalese were repatriated.

One important difference between the violence that took place in Senegal versus that in Mauritania involved the attitude of the local authorities. In Mauritania, the government and security forces were directly implicated in the attacks against blacks -- haratines were seen using military trucks, and the police force did nothing to stop the violence. The Senegalese police, on the other hand, may have been guilty of inefficiency and negligence, but do not appear to have been directly involved in the attacks against Mauritanians. However, the Mauritanian authorities contend that the Senegalese government contributed to the violence by fanning an atmosphere of growing hostility against Mauritania and Moors in Senegal since 1987, that the Senegalese police actually encouraged the attacks against Moors, and that Senegalese officials incited the violence in Dakar by manipulating public anger.

FORCIBLE EXPULSIONS

The rioting and killing in both countries in April 1989 that culminated in the air bridge were but a prologue to the massive campaign against blacks in Mauritania that followed: The Mauritanian government took advantage of the airlifts to begin a systematic expulsion of its black citizens into Senegal, forcing them to leave by air or across the river. Those driven out of their country include intellectuals, civil servants, professionals, businessmen, militant trade unionists, those suspected of opposition, as well as farmers and cattle-herders

---

[5]Doyle, "Blood Brothers," p. 16.

from the Senegal River Valley. The government has sought to justify the mass expulsions as a measure to "repatriate" Senegalese who had obtained Mauritanian nationality through fraudulent means or to expel certain people whose security it could not guarantee. The first secretary of the Mauritanian Embassy in Dakar, Bilal Ould Werzeg, was quoted in *The New York Times* as saying that only Senegalese nationals were being expelled, and that many had fraudulently obtained Mauritanian papers. He also remarked: "No matter what identity card or passport you have, it's where you come from that matters."[6] He acknowledged, however, that lists of suspected Senegalese had been compiled by the police, and that "of course, some mistakes occur, but we're doing all we can to prevent them."

It is abundantly clear, however, that the government expelled thousands of bona fide Mauritanians, using the turmoil created by the conflict and the international airlift scheme as an opportunity to reduce Mauritania's black population. Expulsions of nationals or non-nationals violates international human rights law. For example, Article 12 of the African Charter on Human and Peoples' Rights, ratified by Mauritania on June 26, 1986, states: "The mass expulsion of non-nationals shall be prohibited. Mass expulsion shall be that which is aimed at national, racial, ethnic or religious groups."

It appears that the government's aim was to reduce the political significance of the black population. The expulsion of the blacks served two purposes: it reduced their numbers, especially the numbers of educated blacks, and it reduced the possibility of collaboration between blacks and haratines, thereby lessening the danger that the haratines' political allegiances could desert their erstwhile white Moor masters.

One refugee in Ndiawar explained why he believed that the Mauritanian government's actions were intentional:

> On the whole, it was very important to distance black Mauritanians from the black world, especially from Senegal where the links were very profound and long-standing. This in a way is the one thing that one can say was premeditated and well-prepared. While some of the things that happened after 1989 were in reaction to certain unexpected events, the need to isolate blacks and cut them off from the black world really is the one thing that underlies the government's policy

---

[6]Kenneth B. Noble, "An African Exodus with Racial Overtones," *The New York Times*, July 22, 1989.

> and which was premeditated. There were so many exactions in the valley, people being beaten, killed, etc., that one cannot just say that events of 1989 happened from nowhere in a vacuum. Since 1987, whenever Senegalese came to Mauritania, they were expected to go to the police station and to leave their identity cards there until the persons left, and there were endless questions about why they came, what they were doing there, and about their movements. They could be stopped in the city and then, perhaps because they wouldn't have their identity card, arrested as a delinquent.[7]

The exact number of expulsions is not known. The determination of that number is complicated by the fact that hundreds of blacks fled Mauritania to escape persecution. The United Nations High Commissioner for Refugees (UNHCR) estimates that, as of June 1991, there were 52,995 Mauritanian refugees in Senegal; in June 1993, 52,945 were registered. Most observers agree that the true number is substantially higher, since the UNHCR figure reflects only those refugees who have formally registered with the local authorities, and does not take into account the thousands living with relatives on the Senegalese side of the river and in cities throughout Senegal. A smaller number of refugees have also fled into Mali; the official figure for those who have been registered there is about 13,000, but again, the real number is undoubtedly much higher because of the ease of integration into the life of local communities in Mali.

The first phase of the expulsions in Mauritania generally followed three patterns: expulsions of entire villages in the south; expulsion of Peul herders; and selective expulsions in the cities.

Villages in the South

In the villages in the south, security forces expelled blacks indiscriminately, sometimes forcing entire communities to cross the Senegal River into Senegal. (See the chapter entitled "Land.") Security forces encircled villages, destroyed the inhabitants' identity cards, confiscated their livestock and their belongings, and forced them into boats that took them to the Senegalese bank of the river. Those who resisted or who tried to flee with their belongings were arrested, imprisoned, and sometimes executed.

---

[7]Interview in Senegal, May 1990.

Entire villages in the south were burned or destroyed by the army.[8] A relief worker who was from the area and who travelled there in November 1990 commented on the breadth of the destruction:

> From the areas of Brakna to Selibaby, I counted about thirty villages that had been emptied of Halpulaars. Some of these are now inhabited by Moors; many have been burned and emptied. In some villages, such as Nima and Gourel Gobi (near Djowol), Moors have moved in and are cultivating the land. When I saw what had happened, I was completely depressed. It was such a strong feeling of social injustice.[9]

In the regions of Brakna, Trarza, and Selibaby, numerous villages were "emptied" of their former inhabitants and are now populated by Moors. According to one refugee: "There are wives here whose husbands are over there; husbands whose wives have remained on the other side of the river. Brothers and fathers and sons are separated from each other."[10]

Ahmed, a cultivator and shepherd, was expelled from Brakna, together with about 400 other people. He described the abuses and tragedy they suffered when they were expelled.

> Three girls drowned. One of them was my twelve-year-old daughter, and the other two were eleven-year-old girls whose families were our neighbors. We were in our village when the gendarmes came, accompanied by haratines and white Moors armed with guns, axes, and knives. They gathered our belongings and put about fifty or sixty of us -- men, women, and children -- in a truck. We were searched thoroughly and stripped of our clothes. Men were left in their underpants and shirts, and women in their petticoats. They

---

[8]According to the Union of Democratic Forces (UFD), the main opposition party, the number of destroyed or abandoned villages along the River Valley after the expulsions is as follows: in the region of Trarza, thirty-four; in Gorgol, 103; in Brakna, seventy-four; in Assaba, forty; in Guidimakha, twenty-five.

[9]Interview in New York, March 21, 1991.

[10]Interview in Garly, Senegal, May 27, 1990.

> even took our shoes. We were taken to the gendarmerie where we were stripped. We were then taken to the river. As there were no boats on the Mauritanian side, we were told to swim. The old people who couldn't swim had to be carried by the men. I had to carry my own father.
>
> We were deported on June 27 [1989]. On June 28, the bodies of the three girls were discovered at different points of the river. We then went on to Djoude, and stayed there for two months and then came here.[11]

In an interview with Human Rights Watch/Africa, two women from Gnawlé described the expulsion of residents of their village. The following is a composite testimony of the women.

> We were not given any warning about what was in store for us. Sixty-four heavily armed soldiers came very early in the morning and encircled the village. At 8:00 A.M., the men were called to a "meeting" and they were kept in a tent. At 10:00 A.M., the women were summoned. We refused, saying that our men had been detained since the morning and had not even been allowed to eat breakfast. In protest at their confinement, the men left the tent. The military blocked them and held their guns in position. We knew that the objective was to deport us. They requested military reinforcements. They made the entire village sit in the sun the whole day, with nothing to eat. At 6:00 P.M., the reinforcements arrived. Among the reinforcements was a haratine who spoke to us discreetly. He told us not to resist deportation because of the risk that we would be killed. He said he could offer us no protection, just advice. After that, the whole village agreed that we had no choice but to leave together. However, they selected only the men and held the women back.
>
> There was a very old man, seventy-eight, who had his glasses deliberately broken. They made the men cross and brutalized the women. They took a lot of the young women away to be raped and they brought them back. The women they didn't want, they took off

---

[11]Interview in Senegal, May 1990.

> their top clothes. The younger ones were left only in flimsy tops. Then the women and children were driven in trucks to Salinde, about one hundred kilometers away, to board the boats. When we crossed, we were taken by some Senegalese villagers to the bank opposite our village.[12]

A refugee told Human Rights Watch/Africa of the expulsion on December 22, 1989, of a village that contained approximately nine families, with about eight people in each:

> At about 3:00 P.M., the entire village was told to come to a meeting for a head count. We were all told to bring our I.D.s and all other documents testifying to our civil status in order to determine the false ones. When we all gathered, many of the I.D.s, birth certificates, and other documents were confiscated. We were then told that all the people whose I.D.s were not confiscated could go home, and the other were ordered to remain behind.
>
> The men whose documents had been confiscated or who did not have an I.D. were then accompanied by three gendarmes, two members of the National Guard and several policemen and escorted to their homes. When we got there, each man had to give a detailed account of all the members of his household. Every member of the family had to come out of their house as they were dressed. Those wearing nice clothes were told to take them off and to hand over their watches. Any women wearing gold also had to hand it over. The families were then told to get into trucks. They were driven to the river bank at a place called Deamil, about fifteen kilometers away, and made to cross. At gunpoint, we were then told to get into boats and to swim across. Not everyone could swim and the old people had an especially hard time. Several people drowned.[13]

Peul Herders

The vast majority of those expelled were Peul herders. According to a study conducted by Christian Santoir for the French research company,

---

[12] Interview in Fondé Ass, Senegal, May 25, 1990.

[13] Interview in Senegal, May 1990.

ORSTOM,[14] 67 percent of the Peul encampments on the right bank of the Senegal River were emptied of their former inhabitants by August 1990. The study indicates that some 21,500 Peuls were expelled, which accounts for at least 57 percent of the Peul population of the departments of Kaedi, Monguel, Mbout and Maghama. These figures are undoubtedly too low, since the study was conducted in the department of Matam in Senegal, and does not include the Peuls who fled to other parts of Senegal or to Mali.

The Peuls were targeted in part for economic reasons; their animals were a tangible asset that brought immediate wealth to beydane herders. The animals were often viewed as "compensation" for the Mauritanian-owned boutiques that had been pillaged in Dakar. The majority of the Moors had been nomadic herders themselves until the drought of the 1970s, and they were often more interested in livestock than in land. In addition, while not owning significant agricultural land, the herders benefitted from their access to some of the best remaining pastures as well as to water sources in the river valley.

Traditionally, the Peuls have sought to distance themselves from administrative centers in order to avoid various forms of control and taxation. They have moved their herds from one side of the Senegal River to the other, taking advantage of seasonal changes to secure adequate pastures for the animals. The Mauritanian bank, with its sparser population, is better for herding in times of some rain, while the opposite bank can be relied upon for grazing in periods of drought. Accordingly, after the 1972 drought, many Peul and Moor herders crossed the river to Senegal and Mali. This pattern of Peuls circulating among the three countries bordering the Senegal River -- Mauritania, Senegal, and Mali -- made it more difficult for the Peuls to establish their national identity once the expulsions began. The Mauritanian authorities exploited this to justify the expulsion of Peuls. On the other hand, Moor herders who also had circulated to and from Senegal and Mali were not subject to the same difficulties.

Finally, the Peul herders tended to live in small isolated encampments, each comprised of a few families, scattered over a large areas (particularly in the departments of Kaedi, Monguel, Maghama, and Mbout). Because of their isolation, they were easier to attack and expel than were the more established, sedentary villages. The gendarmes and the army frequently staged surprise attacks and expelled Peuls.

The attacks on Peul encampments by the Mauritanian security forces were

[14] Christian Santoir, "Le Repli Peul en Mauritanie à l'Ouest de l'Assaba," ORSTOM Dakar, January 1991.

usually violent and involved considerable looting and pillaging. The men were tied up, beaten, and then expelled, which ensured that families would be scattered. Those who attempted to escape were shot. The military attackers included haratines, who systematically looted and then frequently burned what was left of the encampment. Once assembled for expulsion, the Peuls' remaining belongings were confiscated -- jewelry, identity papers and documents, and sometimes clothing.[15]

Resistance to attack was met with harsh reprisals, as exemplified by the case of two brothers, Yoro and Abdramane Lam, herders from the area of Foum Gleita. In June 1989, the brothers tried to prevent gendarmes from confiscating their cattle. Yoro was detained without charge or trial, and Abdramane was killed. Their family was expelled to Senegal.[16]

Cities

In the larger towns and cities, the authorities targeted black civil servants, employees of private institutions, trade unionists, former political prisoners and, in some instances, the wives of political prisoners.

In the main cities, such as Nouakchott and Nouadhibou, black civil servants -- including teachers, army officers, policemen, and those working in private enterprise -- were summoned by the police, interrogated, and forced to relinquish their identity cards. They were then transported in trucks, with or without their families, to the bank of the river where boats took them to Senegal. A number of them died, apparently as a result of the severe overcrowding in the trucks, including the case of two people who are said to have died from suffocation in a small van that was carrying thirty people who were being taken from Nouakchott to Rosso for expulsion. Among those expelled in 1989 were Kane Ndiawar, a former advisor to President Taya, and Bâ Abdoul, the director of an important fishing company in Nouadhibou. Trade unionists belonging to the hydro-electric company of Nouadhibou and to the Social Security Office of Nouakchott were also expelled in early May 1989. A number of black diplomats serving abroad were recalled, stripped of their

---

[15] Christian Santoir, "Les Peuls 'Refuse': Les Peul Mauritaniens Refugies au Senegal," ORSTOM Dakar, December 1990.

[16] Amnesty International, *Mauritania: Human Rights Violations in the Senegal River Valley*, October 1990.

credentials, and then expelled.[17]

The urban expulsions were clearly focused on the actual and potential leadership of the black community. A former student at the University of Nouakchott explained that students were particularly targeted:

> In spite of the large number of people affected by the deportations, nonetheless, they were selective enough to ensure that a disproportionate number of them were students. Clearly, they want to break the back of the black community and to deprive them of their educated elements. They also know that we would have financial problems continuing our education even if we are able to register in foreign universities. Most of the students who have come have not been able to continue their studies and even those who are now in university or school lost time and had to repeat at least one year.[18]

Another category that was targeted was civil servants. One refugee told Human Rights Watch/Africa about how one such group was imprisoned and ultimately expelled:

> Just after the conflict started, during the Idd-el-Fitr [the feast at the end of Ramadan], all the black civil servants, six of them, working in the department of Moudjerea were detained for four days there. They were told that they had to be interrogated to see if they were Senegalese. [The names of the six have been withheld because their families are still living in Mauritania. They included teachers and a postal worker.] They were taken to the capital of the region, Tidjikdja, and interrogated. They were then asked to go back to their posts, except those working in Tidjikdja and the surrounding areas, who remained in prison for another three weeks to one month.
>
> Then suddenly those sent back were collected by the governor, as well as other professionals, including nurses and teachers. They

---

[17] Mohammed Athié, a black Mauritanian who served in the Mauritanian Embassy in Washington D.C., was recalled to Nouakchott in May 1989. Instead of returning, he obtained asylum in the U.S.

[18] Interview in Dakar, Senegal, May 1990.

> were taken to the gendarmerie at Moudjeri to be deported on May 31, which was in a few days. Between thirty and forty of us (excluding our families) were put into one truck and taken to a camp in Boghe. We were taken to a big hall and searched one by one, and deprived of all the possessions we had on, including watches, chains, some radios, shoes, and *boubous* [clothing]. We were given a shirt and trousers. Our identity papers were also confiscated; we were put in a *pirogue* [canoe] and sent to Senegal.
>
> All of us are 100 percent Mauritanian. Most of us have our great-great-great grandparents buried in Mauritania. Many of them said they had never seen the river.[19]

Zeinaba, a thirty-year-old civil servant who was expelled from the town of Selibaby where she worked, described the systematic operation:

> I was not the only black civil servant deported at the time from Selibaby. There were 128 persons deported in the first wave on May 6. Ninety civil servants were also dismissed.[20]

The expulsions from the cities were equally as arbitrary and abusive as those from the rural areas. A woman who was working in Nouadhibou at the time of her expulsion explained:

> I had just come to the office and had just withdrawn my salary when I realized that a member of the Brigade was following me. He told me to give the money back as I was not a Mauritanian. He arrested me on the spot; he would not even allow me to go home to fetch the children. Fortunately, our family knew some of his colleagues and persuaded him to let me collect the children. He took my I.D. and tore it up in front of me. I was breast-feeding a seven-month-old baby at the time. Since they drove me to the house to collect the children, they were able to recognize it and I learned later that they went back and took everything. We had to wait all night for a plane.

---

[19]Interview in Dakar, Senegal, May 13, 1990.

[20]Interview in Dagana, Senegal, May 25, 1990.

> We were finally put directly onto an airplane and arrived in Dakar.[21]

Wives of black political prisoners were also targeted for expulsion. Their cases are particularly tragic because not only did they endure surveillance, harassment, and marginalization because of their husbands' imprisonment, but they also were forcibly expelled without any possibility of contacting their husbands. Among the cases in 1989 of expulsion of wives of political prisoners were the following.

- Aissatou Ly, whose husband Moussa Ly was a businessman from Nouadhibou who was imprisoned in September 1986. (Her husband is one of those believed to have died in detention in 1991.)

- Djeinaba Kane, the wife of Harouna Kane, an army officer who was imprisoned in late 1987, was also expelled.

- Faty Kamar, the wife of Haby Toumbou, who was in prison at the time she was expelled. She had been working for the National Mining and Industrial Company (SNIM) in Nouadhibou.

- Habsa Banon was a customs official and the wife of Ibrahima Sall who was still in prison. On May 29, 1989, she was kidnapped in the street and expelled, leaving her three children, aged between seven and twelve, in Nouakchott. The children were only able to join her in Senegal two months later.[22]

ABUSES ASSOCIATED WITH EXPULSIONS

Apart from the fact that summary expulsion is a gross abuse of human rights in itself, the whole process of expulsion involved numerous abuses against the expellees. Some of the abuses were perpetrated systematically by the government and its security forces; others were committed by individuals with at least the implicit sanction of the government and complete impunity.

In several villages and in the cities, security forces are reported to have tortured people for weeks before actually expelling them. People were beaten

[21]Interview in Senegal, May 1990.

[22]Interview with Habsa Banon, November 8, 1991, Paris, France.

after they had been hand-cuffed and had their feet tied together. Some were denied food for two or three days. Others were subjected to a form of torture known as the "jaguar."[23] These and other abuses are detailed in the following section.

The testimony of Imam Mohamed El Faso, an Imam [Islamic religious leader] in Aleg, illustrates the range of abuses committed during the expulsions:

> I am not the only imam to be deported. Many other black imams have been deported. What is the most shocking is not that imams were deported, but the terrible abuses, the massacres, rape, and burning of homes, etc., against ordinary people who are muslims and the violation to Islam itself.
>
> On May 10, a group of beydanes leading haratines came to our house. The haratines directed by the beydanes took everything they could lay their hands on. What they could not take, they destroyed. I had two large trunks full of Islamic books, including many copies of the Koran. They burned everything in front of my eyes. That of course hurt me the most and they knew that. They came beating war-drums. For them it was a war. On May 10, my house was burned to the ground. Aleg is a regional capital and there are rows of houses next to each other. But they were selective about choosing only black houses. My house was only 200 meters from the office and home of the governor of the region, which made it easy to see the extent of government complicity in these operations.
>
> That first day, I personally knew of twenty-two people who were seriously injured with broken limbs and fractures. At the hospital, they were not given any treatment. When our homes were attacked the head of the regional police, the commander of the gendarmerie, the regional military commander and the director of the Regional Security Services were all there but they never intervened or helped the victims. They only intervened when a black attempted to defend himself. They confiscated his weapon and arrested him. Some of

[23]"Jaguar" is a form a torture where the victim is hung over an iron bar with his hands and feet tied together, and is turned on the bar and beaten. Water is thrown on him, and he is subjected to more beatings.

the people arrested at the time in Aleg have never been heard of again. Others were arrested and then deported. Others were promised to be released if they paid and were deported after they paid.

On May 22, there was another attack in Aleg followed by a new wave of arrests. The attack followed the same pattern as above. Among those arrested were:

Ousmane Diop, a baker;
Amadou N'diaye, an inspector;
Thierno Alassane, a marabout [religious leader];
Sow Abou, a pharmacist;
Mboth, a policeman;
Bâ Mamadou Pathie, a trader;
Bâ Ibrahim, a local government employee;
Diallo Moctar, school director.

They were imprisoned at the police station for eight days without being given anything to eat. Their families were collected and spent the night at the station. At the police station, all their valuables including, watches and jewelry, were taken. From there, they were piled on top of each other in trucks and taken to Boghé. They had nothing but what they were wearing.

At Boghé, those who had on *boubous* were stripped. People took what they wanted and the rest were burned in a heap. From Boghé, we left in another truck and put on boats across the river. We went first to Demele and came here with the help of the Red Cross. We were expelled on May 27.[24]

Detentions Prior to Expulsion

Detention prior to expulsion was perhaps the most common abuse. Many blacks were summoned by police for interrogation when the decision was made to expel them. Prominent citizens, whom the authorities assumed would not try to run away, were often requested to come to the station for questioning every

[24]Interview in Dakar, Senegal, May 14, 1990.

day for several weeks.

Many of the testimonies in this chapter allude to the detentions prior to expulsion. A thirty-five-year-old sailor working in Nouadhibou, Mauritania's principal commercial port, told Human Rights Watch/Africa about his experience at several detention sites:

> I was taken to the central police station in Nouadhibou, and detained there for a month and ten days. After three days, the commissioner said he had received orders from above that I was not to be given the food brought by relatives. Sometimes, I ate nothing for three to four days, and even then, only what the black guards could sneak in. Then, I was transferred to the central police station in Nouakchott and detained for twenty-five days. Then I was driven in the direction of Rosso, and a lot of money I had on me was taken.
>
> At Khare, I was told that since I was well-built, I should carry the old people across, When I said that I could not carry them all, the gendarmes threatened to shoot me.[25]

Oumar was a student at the Scientific Institute in Nouakchott who was expelled together with his mother and sixteen-year-old sister. He described the detention of his elderly father:

> First, my seventy-two-year-old father was arrested on December 3, 1989, and detained without charge for three months in the police station of the fifth district. He was arrested again two weeks after his release. We have no idea where he is being held or even if he is still alive. He is in poor health; during the three months of his detention, his hands and feet were tied up and, as a result, he has problems with his back and feet.
>
> A few days after my father's second arrest, my mother was arrested in early April. She was told to report to the police station every evening from 6:00–9:00 P.M. until the day of our deportation.[26]

---

[25]Interview in Senegal, May 1990.

[26]Interview in Senegal, May 1990.

Sexual Harassment

Women were often subject to sexual harassment and even rape before expulsion, especially while in detention. Because of the shame associated with sexual abuses, Human Rights Watch/Africa was not able to gather much testimony from victims.

A former official in the Ministry of Education who was dismissed as part of the purge of black professionals, described her experience of sexual harassment:

> I was arrested on March 27 in Nouakchott and taken to the state security headquarters.... I was kept there for forty-eight hours and interrogated about my origins. They kept my identity papers, and for the next month, I had to report every day to their office and remain there from 8:00 A.M to 3:00 P.M. Officials try to take advantage when they see a woman sitting there; they come to your house in the evening to pester you.
>
> From April 27 until my expulsion, I was detained in the central police station of the Judiciary Police, together with another woman and five men who were all deported. Women detained in police stations run a serious risk of being raped and are constantly subject to degrading treatment. Food was very scarce and medical attention non-existent. You are very isolated because other blacks are afraid to visit you for fear of being arrested themselves.
>
> The day of our deportation, we were called one by one to the office of the director and, in front of everyone, were told to undress just to humiliate us. Everyone's watches and jewelry were taken; when they failed to remove my bracelet, they broke it in half.[27]

Other testimonies obtained by Human Rights Watch/Africa indicate that this experience was not unusual. A former employee of the U.S. embassy described the last stages of the treatment of a group of detainees before they were expelled:

> They took us to a cereal warehouse and made us sit down in a filthy

---

[27]Interview in Senegal, May 1990.

> corner for five hours. At 9:00 P.M., we had to take the *pirogue* to cross. There was a customs officer who terrorized everyone; he was especially hard on the women. The women were searched with a vindictiveness that was shameful, including their private parts. Several women were raped.[28]

Theft of Possessions

Before the blacks were expelled, police and security forces usually confiscated their belongings -- money, jewelry, clothing, food, and any other valuables. Earrings were taken out of women's ears, clothing removed from the backs of young and old, even family photographs were confiscated. Most deportees lost everything they owned.

Human Rights Watch/Africa was told of many cases in which the security forces stole the possessions of expellees. Two examples will suffice to illustrate. Zeinaba, a civil servant, told Human Rights Watch/Africa in an interview in May 1990:

> I arrived in Senegal on May 6, 1989. I was living in Selibaby. They came to my office on May 5 to arrest me. I lived near the police station and so when they brought me there, my older brother and three children came to the station, including the baby who my brother carried. At the station, Menim ould Mohamed Talib, the commissioner, took my bracelet, earrings, my necklace (gold), all the money in my bank account and even my *boubou* and shoes, leaving me wearing a slip. That is how I arrived in Senegal -- in a slip.
>
> After I was deported, my eldest child, a ten-year-old girl, was interrogated for two days for the purpose of identifying where I had left my jewelry and money. Then the girl herself was deported, on her own. My nine-year old daughter and baby boy, who was four months old, are in Mauritania with my in-laws. My husband was studying abroad at the time. My daughter and I eventually found each other in Bakel; at the shock of seeing her, I fainted and was hospitalized for ten days for heart trouble.[29]

---

[28]Interview in Senegal, May 1990.

[29]Interview in Dagana, Senegal, May 25, 1990.

A former employee of the U.S. Embassy in Nouakchott, who was expelled from Rosso while visiting relatives, was interviewed in Rosso on May 28, 1990. He stated:

> At 2:30 P.M., several policemen came to my house.... Two policemen were left to watch over us, as the others went through our cupboards and our belongings. The most shocking was when the Police Commissioner asked me personally if our TV was black and white or color. I did not respond. We were then ordered to get into a police car. I asked where we were going and the Commissioner replied: "to join your father Abdou Diouf [the president of Senegal]."
>
> Our eight children were not in the house at the time. I said I could not go anywhere without my children. He replied that I need not worry about them since "they were Mauritanians, and not Senegalese." Eventually, he allowed us to gather our children. To our shock, the Commissioner then asked the children to take their clothes off, on the basis that "they were bought with Mauritanian and not Senegalese money," implying that I was a Senegalese who had taken advantage of Mauritania.

Since the mass expulsions began, blacks have carried their money on their persons, for fear that they would not be able to retrieve it from the bank or that their houses would be broken into and their valuable and cash taken in their absence in the search for "Senegalese" residents.

Confiscation of Land

One of the major aims of the expulsions was to accelerate the process of land confiscation already underway in the Senegal River Valley. According to a Mauritanian exile:

> The Moors lost goods in Senegal, and they wanted compensation. That's why they went after the herds of the Peuls -- some were eaten, some were sold and some were kept as herds. It was almost an accident that the Peuls were targeted. But the government's long term policy was focused on land. And they had ways of getting that land.[30]

---

[30]Interview in Dakar, Senegal, March 6, 1991.

The forcible expulsions were also a response to the increasing difficulty of confiscating land, as the confiscations moved into the middle areas of the river valley. A former resident of Selibaby described how the expulsions were used to get land in his region.

> In the region of Guidimaka, many Soninkés refused to give up their land. The authorities tried to force them to sell it and to work for the new owners. The only solution was to expel them. Haratines now work that land. I can see them working in the fields on the other side of the river.[31]

The expulsions radically changed the character of land ownership along the valley: Entire villages containing hundreds of people were summarily expelled to Senegal; others fled in fear for their lives; hundreds were imprisoned or killed. One relief worker who knew the river valley well and returned to the area several months after the deportations began described the scene as "macabre."

The expulsions enabled the beydanes to take over the land formerly held by blacks. In some instances, haratines work the land now owned by beydane businessmen; in other cases, Moors repatriated from Senegal were given land to cultivate.

The haratines played an important part in the land seizures after the expulsions began. The haratines were used by the government to carry out much of the violence associated with the expulsions, and they were often given a share in the booty, namely, the goods confiscated from the deportees. According to an elderly refugee in Garly:

> Haratines were brought in specifically to loot the houses and they took smaller items. The authorities confiscated all the livestock and other valuables belonging to everyone who had been deported.[32]

The beydane authorities realized that giving land to the haratines would be helpful in cementing their political allegiance. This effort to separate the haratines from the ethnic black populations was crucial to the government's strategy. Samba, a refugee from Selibaby, described how the haratines treated

---

[31]Interview in Dar es Salaam, Department of Bakel, Senegal, February 27, 1991.

[32]Interview in Garly, Senegal, May 1990.

the villagers:

> The haratines were told that they could do whatever they wanted, so they took our things, beat people, stole our animals. All this was done to sow terror in us. Finally, we were forbidden even to leave the village; we couldn't cultivate our fields -- haratines were cultivating our land. We couldn't take it any more. We had to leave.[33]

Human Rights Watch/Africa has obtained many testimonies of black farmers whose land was confiscated by means of expelling the owners. One such case, that of a man from the village of Beylane, illustrates the process:

> I had two fields -- one of maize and one of sorghum. In 1989, a beydane came and measured my field. He was accompanied by a delegation, made up of a gendarme, the district supervisor, the prefect, and the governor. I went and asked them what was going on, but they wouldn't respond. Two weeks later, the beydane marked off the land with cement blocks. I made an appointment to see the district supervisor but the day we were supposed to meet, I was forced to cross the river.[34]

A man from the village of Chapsabel described a similar experience at his cooperative, which typifies the experience of many black farmers:

> Our cooperative had seventy-seven members and several fields on the river, including a rice-paddy of twenty-seven hectares. In late 1988 or early 1989, Moors -- civilians and gendarmes -came with measuring sticks. We asked why, and they said that the land belongs to the state. They took three maize fields, about ten hectares, and four fields of millet. Finally, in May the gendarmes said that the whole village had to leave.[35]

---

[33]Interview outside Bakel, Senegal, February 27, 1991.

[34]Interview in Beylane, Senegal, March 1, 1991.

[35]Interview in Beylane, Senegal, March 1, 1991.

Destruction of Legal Documents

During the expulsions, virtually all identity papers -- including national I.D. cards, birth certificates, diplomas, and professional identification papers -- were systematically seized and destroyed. Most expellees are therefore unable to prove their Mauritanian citizenship, their title to land or other property, or the particulars of their employment. The confiscation of such documents belonging to a group of farmers was detailed in the above testimonies. Another case is described by a former employee of the U.S. Embassy in Nouakchott:

> Five hundred and fifty-nine of us were deported on May 6, 1989. The majority were women whose husbands had been deported and children without either parent. At 2:30 P.M., several policemen came to my house. I had left Nouakchott to spend festivities in my village. When the police arrived, my brother and I were together. They asked for my I.D. and they took it, together with my certificate of nationality. My brother and my wife handed over their I.D.s as well. They stated that our documents were not authentic.

Ousmane, a refugee in Dakar, described the problems faced by blacks who were fired after the expulsions began, blocked from withdrawing their savings from the bank, and forced to leave the cities and return to their villages.

> Those dismissed had problems when they sought to leave Nouakchott and go to the valley, which most had to do for economic reasons. The police manning the control system know that these people are in trouble with the government. They try to extort a bribe from you, threatening your children. There are other threats. As a matter of routine, blacks are asked to get off public transportation and to show their I.D. cards, which are usually confiscated and torn up, saying that they are fake, and that the blacks are trafficking in national papers.[36]

Any attempts to make legal challenges to the expulsions were fruitless. A lawyer interviewed by Human Rights Watch/Africa in Dakar who had been expelled from Nouakchott in June 1989, described his experience, which illustrates the Mauritanian government's contempt for legality:

---

[36]Interview in Dakar, Senegal, June 5, 1990.

I was with my family at the time that the events between Senegal and Mauritania broke out. I then came back to Nouakchott, and two days later I learned that the police had come to my office. I went straightaway to the police station to find out why they had come. The police commissioner gave my name and asked if I was that person. He then told me to come back that same evening with my diplomas.

I came back to the police station with the relevant papers as well as with the document proving my civil status, copies of my diplomas, etc. They said that they thought I had done my studies in Senegal, but in fact I had studied in Iraq. They said that because my identity card was issued in 1975 it must by necessity be fraudulent. Of course, in a country like Mauritania it is not automatic that people register for identity cards. They do so only when they need it for state purposes such as going to a modern school, but of course the overwhelming number of people, especially in the 1960s, 1970s and before that, went to Koranic schools and did not need official papers.

Someone from the bar association came to collect me and then the next day I was told to come back to the police station and to wait outside. I learned then that the director of regional security had told all the other people who were also there to go, except for me. The central police station in Nouakchott was then given the order to expel me. It was made clear to them that this should be done quickly in order to avoid negative publicity, because people were coming to find out why I was being detained and why the fuss was being made about my identity card on the basis that it had been issued in 1975. I was then told to bring someone who could prove that I was Mauritanian: I refused to do so on the basis that the tribunal which issued me with this identity card in itself represented the people of Mauritania as a whole, therefore I did not see the necessity to bring one person along to testify to what a tribunal representing the nation had decided in my favor.

I was then taken to the police station in the fourth district of Nouakchott where I was asked details about my bank accounts and other possessions: I refused to reply. They also wanted to confiscate my professional card. Of course as lawyers, we know the techniques

> of the police very well. We also know many policemen individually and therefore they hesitated to search me. When they established a list of about a hundred people who were all waiting at the police station in the fourth district who were to be deported, they summoned a car and that same day we were driven to Rosso where we arrived before 10:00 P.M. the same night.[37]

The combination of systematic discrimination and lack of legal documents have led to the denial of many civil rights to blacks.

Since the expulsions began, blacks have had great difficulty in obtaining identity cards and even in renewing them after they expire. The same is true for passports and other government-issued papers.

Freedom of movement within the country is also restricted. Blacks describe continual harassment at the numerous checkpoints along the major roads. Whether they are in private cars or using public transportation, blacks are singled out by the military and police, often forced to show their identification papers and the contents of their luggage, and sometimes detained.

Settling Private Scores

The existing climate of persecution of blacks has had another effect -- allowing beydanes to exploit the government's policies in order to settle private scores. Such exploitation has been used to dispossess black farmers of their land, to cripple black business competition, and to interrupt payment to black employees and domestic servants and facilitate their expulsion if they insist on getting paid. One observer, a medical doctor, described the massive dismissal of blacks from their jobs as an "economic embargo." He continued:

> Health workers were also affected by these measures. Nurses, for example, were told not to come to work until they got new orders. A week later, they would hear on the radio that they had been fired for abandoning their posts without explanation.[38]

The following case is typical of the many testimonies gathered by Human Rights Watch/Africa that illustrate how the process often worked:

---

[37]Interview in Dakar, Senegal, March 1991.

[38]Interview in Dakar, Senegal, February 24, 1991.

Djeinaba (a pseudonym) was working in Nouakchott in a private enterprise. She went to see her employer in Nouadhibou when her supervisor failed to pay her for ten consecutive months. Negotiations involving the police resulted in an agreement that she would be reimbursed in three installments on specified dates. She never received the money. Shortly after the first date, the police came to arrest her. They said that, according to the supervisor, she was a Senegalese who had been expelled and had returned and was threatening her. On that basis, she was to be expelled. She described her deportation.

> I was locked up in a cell as if I were a thief. When my relatives came to visit me, I was not allowed to see them. Instead, they were interrogated about our family's origins and questioned about their ties to me. A few days later, my mother, who is mauresque [a Moor], traveled from Nouakchott to visit me, and she too had to answer the same questions. She had to bring all her identity papers to prove the link between us. The police took my certificate of nationality and my birth certificate, and those belonging to my mother, to the mayor's office to see if it were possible that I could be the daughter of a mauresque. After a month and three days, my mother was told that I was going to be sent to Nouakchott for further inquiries. She left for Nouakchott and I was transferred there.
>
> I was held at the central police station and asked the same questions about my family's origins. I stayed there for a month and seventeen days. I know my mother came to visit me but I was not allowed to see her; I had to share the food she brought me with the guards. I was only allowed to go to the toilet at specific times. The day before my deportation, my mother was told to come back the next day in order to sign a paper for my release; by the time she came, I had already been transferred. That same day, the policemen tore up, in my presence, my birth certificate and my certificate of nationality. They took my jewelry and my clothes.
>
> I don't know what I am doing here. I was born in Senegal, my family moved to Mauritania when I was three months old and I have had nothing to do with Senegal; I have never even visited it before.[39]

[39]Interview in Senegal, May 1990.

The expulsions vastly accelerated the government's campaign to eradicate black business competition. The targeted destruction of black-owned businesses during the events of April 1989, combined with the persistent refusal of banks to provide loans and credits to blacks, served to strangle black businesses in Mauritania.

IMPACT OF THE EXPULSIONS

The Mauritanian government seized the opportunity of the April 1989 incidents in Senegal to empty the country of as many black Africans as possible. The intention was to ensure that the Arabization campaign would succeed, that the demographic dominance of the Moors would not be challenged, and that the haratines would not switch their political allegiances from the beydanes to the blacks.

Carried to their logical extreme, the expulsions were meant to change the entire ethnic character of Mauritania. Although not all blacks have been expelled, Mauritania's ethnic composition has markedly changed. Visitors and citizens alike can no longer recognize the country they knew. Ibrahima Sall, one of the 1986 FLAM prisoners (See "Arrest and Detention of Black Activists"), told Human Rights Watch/Africa what it was like when he was released in 1990 after so many of those he knew had been expelled:

> I never thought I would leave prison alive. They said I was the brains [of FLAM]. I had a kind of vertigo, from being used to restricted space. I also had the feeling that I was nothing, that life just continues without you. I didn't believe in the country any more. There was also an emptiness -- my family was gone, my friends had been deported. I saw my mother -- she was eighty-seven years old -- and she didn't recognize me.
>
> I had another shock, when I went to Bogué. I looked at the river through the window of my old room -- I used to always go to bathe in the river, it was a sort of ceremony. And now I couldn't, because of the guards along the river. And then I knew that things had changed.[40]

---

[40]Interview in Paris, France, November 1991.

4
LAND EXPROPRIATION

A principal focus of conflict between the beydanes and the black population of Mauritania has been the land along the Senegal River Valley. This conflict has led to widespread human rights abuses against the indigenous black population by successive Mauritanian governments, acting exclusively in the interests of the beydanes. These abuses have been characterized by the use of violence and a complete disregard for due process.

Human Rights Watch/Africa takes no position on who should have title to the disputed land; rather, we insist that disputes over title and use of land be resolved by peaceful means and with full regard for due process. We believe that governments have obligations in this regard, including: to provide a fair and impartial forum for the settlement of disputes; to avoid and prevent violence by private parties and to prosecute those who resort to such tactics; to prohibit state agents from using unwarranted violence or from circumventing the due process rights of all parties to a dispute.

In the decades since independence, the land of the Senegal River Valley has become an increasingly vital resource, central to the economic future of the country. At independence, control over this land was vested almost entirely in sedentary black communities, chiefly Halpulaar and Soninké farmers, and to a lesser extent in Peul herdsmen, who exercised a variety of traditional tenure rights.

Over the last decade, the beydane-dominated government has tried repeatedly to take over control of the land through a series of measures involving widespread and systematic abuses of human rights. The process started with encouragement by the government to individual beydane entrepreneurs to take the land. It intensified following a land reform proclamation in 1983, which formally vested land ownership in the state and allowed those with preferential access to the state bureaucracy (i.e., the beydanes) to obtain land traditionally occupied by blacks. As explained below, a variety of quasi-legal means were used to seize land. As one refugee in N'Diom explained to Human Rights Watch/Africa: "Even if they don't use force to take the land, the state manages to take it."

The expropriations reached their height in 1989–90, with massive and violent expulsions of entire farming communities along the Senegal River Valley. After the initial expulsions, the military occupation of the valley led to what one Mauritanian exile referred to as "indirect expulsions." In this period, which is still continuing, the military has subjected villagers to a range of abuses, including arbitrary arrest and detention, physical abuse, rape, and widespread looting and pillaging. As the exile explained, "If the people are tired of this abuse by the security forces, the only answer is to flee."

The policy of land expropriation is drastically altering the demographic and economic character of the northern bank of the river. Halpulaar and Soninké farmers and Peul pastoralists are being replaced by new immigrants from the north, namely beydane landowners, their haratine vassals, and a few impoverished communities of indigenous blacks reduced to the status of landless laborers who are working for wages on land that previously belonged to them and their ancestors.

Many blacks who formerly owned and cultivated the land along the Senegal River Valley are now landless laborers. One former farmer explained:

> It's always the same pattern. The government takes the land away from the blacks to give to white Moors, who then ask black Moors [haratines] to work the land. The white Moor gets all the benefits. If you, the former owner, want to work the land, the best of them [white Moor owners] may accept, after long negotiations, that you work a part of the land to help with technical expertise -- this is the exchange. But many of them don't even accept that. There are many arrangements possible between the old and the new master of the land, but one thing remains unchanged, the former owner *loses* his land and nothing can compensate him for that.[1]

Tens of thousands of former farmers are living as refugees in Senegal, and the remainder are living in fear under military occupation, facing an uncertain future.

BACKGROUND: A SOCIAL ORDER UNDER THREAT

At independence, the social and economic core of Mauritania was the raising of livestock. About three-quarters of the population was nomadic, depending almost entirely on animal rearing for sustenance and income. Livestock exports were the main source of foreign exchange, along with the tin and copper mines operated by French companies (located in the north, in beydane territory). Trade, also dominated by the beydanes, was an important source of income. In contrast, the farming communities of the Senegal River

---

[1] Interview in Dagana, Senegal, June 1990.

Valley were both socially and economically marginal.

In the 1970s and 1980s, repeated droughts decimated herds, threatening the viability of nomadic pastoralism and the prospects for the beydanes' continued dominance. In 1972 alone, an estimated 25 percent of the beydanes' animals died. Total herd losses of the order of 80 percent were not uncommon. There was a hemorrhage of destitute nomads to the cities and the farming areas. Impoverished beydanes could no longer afford to keep slaves and vassals, many of whom were emancipated. While many of the beydanes struggled to keep alive their traditional way of life, their former servants often took up new economic opportunities in the towns and in the farming areas.

The great pastoral shake-out of the 1970s saw a corresponding increase in the value of farmland and the agricultural products, since it became increasingly clear that the land along the valley would be critical for the economic future of the country. The nomadic communities of the north, driven south by the drought, were forced to pasture their animals along the Senegal River Valley, on land traditionally owned by the black Peul nomads and the river valley farmers. The beydane nomads were obliged to buy larger quantities of grain, at higher prices. Food became a politically sensitive issue.

The black farmers and herders were not nearly so affected by the drought. Cultivation continued along the river, and many farmers with stores of grain in reserve benefitted from the high cereal prices. Some were able to invest in livestock and challenge the beydanes' domination of the animal market.

Following the 1970s drought, as international aid agencies began to express an interest in the Sahelian region, it became clear that development projects would be concentrated in the high-potential areas, namely the farming areas, especially those close to rivers. In 1972, the governments of Mali, Senegal and Mauritania formed the Organization pour le Mise en Valeur du Fleuve Senegal (OMVS -- the Organization for the Development of the Senegal River) to begin systematic development of the resources of the river valley.

A number of black farmers responded to the drought by migrating to Dakar or France to find work. By the mid-1970s, 65 percent of the estimated 60–70,000 African workers in France were Soninké, with a large representation of Mauritanian Soninké.[2] A further 15 percent were Pulaar. The income from

---

[2] P. Bradley, C. Raynaut and J. Torrealba, *The Guidimaka Region of Mauritania: A Critical Analysis Leading to a Development Project*, London, War on Want, 1977.

Mauritanian expatriates' remittances amounted to 1.45 billion CFA[3] -- larger than the entire foreign aid to the country. This remitted income was directed mostly to Soninké communities, who were able to buy consumer goods and invest in cattle and trade.

By the 1980s, the most precious commodity in Mauritania was riverine farmland. The drought had altered the economy so that control of farmland meant control of the country's food supply, as well as control of the most reliable pastures for animals.

The combination of the remittance income, the selective impact of the drought, and the increasing value of the riverine land strengthened the black communities of the valley vis-á-vis the beydanes, setting the stage for a confrontation. In contrast to the other Sahelian countries, the drought had the effect of threatening to stand the social order on its head.

TRADITIONAL LAND TENURE IN THE SENEGAL RIVER VALLEY

The Senegal River Valley has been inhabited for centuries by indigenous black peoples, though the shifting regional politics over the last two centuries has caused important fluctuations in the patterns of human habitation and cultivation. The tenure system reflected the complex cultivation systems used along the valley. The riverbank itself *(falo)*, which can be cultivated by mechanical irrigation, was the most prized land, with the tightest control. The sandbanks left by the river itself (*waalo*) as it contracted after the rains, which could be cultivated as flood-retreat, required a more subtle system of tenure, as the banks might shift during each rainy season. The majority of the alluvial land (*fonde and waalo*) would be flooded occasionally, depending on the height of the river.[4] Crops would be grown almost entirely on the groundwater retained by the heavy soils, without artificial irrigation. The unpredictability of the flood would mean that certain areas would be either too dry or too waterlogged for cultivation in a certain year, so a land with well-established ownership rights might remain unused for one or more years. Large areas were left uncultivated

---

[3]CFA stands for *Communauté Financière Africaine* (the African Financial Community), whose currency is the CFA franc. The CFA used to be tied to French franc at 50 to 1, but was devalued in January 1994.

[4] John Grayzel, "Land Tenure in Mauritania: The Causes and Consequences of Legal Modernization in a National Context," in R. E. Downs and S. P Reyna (eds.) *Land and Society in Contemporary Africa*, Hanover, Univ. Press of New England, 1988; Bradley *et al.*, 1977.

at any one time. Traditional tenure rights therefore did not observe the indirass principle, found in Islamic law, whereby tenurial rights lapse if the owner fails to cultivate for a certain period of time.

The failure of both the Mauritanian government and advisors to international donor agencies to recognize the complexity of this system of "natural irrigation" became an important factor in the land expropriations of the 1980s (see below).

Under the French colonial administration, traditional tenure rights were generally accepted. These rights were confirmed just before independence by the Decree of 1960 dealing with land tenure. Article 1 of this Decree stated that "Lands that are vacant and without owner belong to the state," but Article 3 stipulated that "customary tenure rights are confirmed when they involve an evident and permanent use of the soil." For the blacks living in the river valley, these measures constituted an important acknowledgement of their right to continue cultivating their lands.

Soon after independence, the government challenged the traditional land tenure system. According to John Grayzel, who has studied land tenure issues in Mauritania:

> In terms of land tenure policy, both *bidan* (beydane) and *haratin* are beginning to be less concerned with maintaining their traditional footholds than with establishing new ones. To do this along the river requires a "de-communitarianization" of land and a new individualistic distribution of land parcels.[5]

The Moors were able benefit from the development policies encouraged by the World Bank and the International Monetary Fund, which encouraged the development of systems of land tenure based on individual private ownership. The donors must have realized that the policies they were encouraging were having a negative effect on the fundamental civil and political rights of the black ethnic groups living in the Senegal River Valley, but considered these problems to be outside the realm of the donors' economic concerns. Accordingly, in contrast to some other African governments, the Mauritanian government was happy to comply with this policy, as described by Prof. Michael Horowitz:

> The expropriation of lands from smallholders found ideological

---

[5] Grayzel, "Land Tenure in Mauritania," p. 328.

> support in the structural adjustment programs of the World Bank, the International Monetary Fund and other multilateral and bilateral donors, who promote the disengagement of the state from direct investments in rural and agricultural development in favor of a more active private sector. In Mauritania, "private sector" refers uniquely to the elite Bidans or white Moors...[6]

In Africa generally, international aid donors have encouraged individual tenure in order to encourage more sustainable land use practices and greater investment in the land. Conflict with traditional land tenure systems has been common. In Mauritania, however, the change to private holdings had an additional and more significant agenda: It facilitated the expropriation of land from black farmers to benefit the ruling beydanes. The Mauritanian government and the beydane-dominated private sector were eager to accept the individual land tenure programs supported by the international donors as a way of providing land holdings to the beydanes at the expense of the rights of other citizens, notably the black ethnic groups. The donors' policies thus provided a cover of respectability for accomplishing this goal by abusive means. A study prepared for the United States Agency for International Development (AID) and the Land Tenure Center of the University of Wisconsin (hereafter, the Park study) supports this analysis, as follows:

> Many residents of the Senegal River Basin feel that the Mauritanian government acceded early to this pressure [for individualized tenure] in large part because an individual tenure policy provided an entry for expanded Bidan land holdings in the Senegal River Basin.[7]

EARLY YEARS OF CONFLICT

The government's interest in the Senegal River Valley was heightened after

---

[6]Michael Horowitz, "Victims Upstream and Down," *The Journal of Refugee Studies*, vol. 4., no. 2, 1991.

[7]Thomas K. Park, Mamadou Baro and Tidiane Ngaido, *Conflicts Over Land and the Crisis of Nationalism in Mauritania*, prepared for USAID and the Land Tenure Center, October 1990, p. 18.

1972, with the creation of the OMVS. By constructing two dams on the river,[8] OMVS aimed to enhance the potential of the Senegal River in terms of irrigation, electricity and navigation. This led to a dramatic increase in the economic value of the land in the valley, and a corresponding increase in the beydanes' interest in the land. In the words of one black Mauritanian:

> With the construction of the dams, the government realized that if the blacks stayed in the valley, they would benefit from the new production capacity of the river. Meanwhile, in the north, there were no further possibilities for irrigation. So the beydanes in the north felt that they had to annex the land that belonged to the blacks in the south. Some blacks tried to sensitize the villagers about what was happening, particularly after 1984; we wanted to help them hold on to their land.[9]

There was another factor that increased the government's interest in the land in the valley -- Mauritania's costly involvement in the war in the Western Sahara. Because of the war, Mauritania increased its armed forces -- from about 3,000 in early 1976 to 15,000–17,000 by mid-1978 -- and found many of the new recruits among the black and haratine populations. The military build-up strained the country's already weak economy, which heightened the government's interest in the river valley for future development. The fighting also led to the displacement of some nomadic Moor communities from the north.

After the war, many of the haratines who were demobilized were interested in the land in the valley. The wish to keep the black and haratine population divided was another source of government interest in the land, as explained by Christian Santoir, a French specialist on the river valley:

> [The army] welcomed a majority of slaves and haratines, who had been freed from their traditional activities by the drought. In 1979, with the resolution of the conflict in Western Sahara (occupied by Morocco), the demobilization began of many the haratines -- without masters, without herds and especially without land. The access to land for this important part of the Mauritanian population, who were

[8]The two dams were Manantali, on the Bafing tributary in Mali, and Diama, at St. Louis in Senegal.

[9]Interview in N'Dioum, Senegal, March 1, 1991.

close to the [white] Moors and shared their culture, would become a permanent concern of the government.[10]

The expropriation of black-owned lands in the Senegal River Valley started well before the land reform legislation of 1983, but initially lacked a legal basis. Confiscation of land began in the area of Rosso in the western valley. Rosso was a logical place to start for several reasons. First, large tracts of land existed. Second, the area was well connected to Nouakchott by excellent roads, so that most of the new proprietors, who were beydane businessmen, could easily travel there and transport their agricultural produce to the city at relatively low cost. Third, the black communities of the area are traditionally less well organized than those further into the interior.

DISCRIMINATORY APPLICATION OF THE LAND REFORM OF 1983

Prior to 1983, there was a clear willingness on the part of the authorities to help beydanes acquire land. However, it was not until after the land reform of 1983 that the government's discriminatory policy of confiscating black lands entered into force. The land reform of 1983 was the legal enactment of the government and beydane's interest in the land of the Senegal River Valley. Ordinance 83.127 of June 5, 1983, nationalized all the land in the country and abolished the traditional systems of land tenure. Selected articles from the ordinance include:

> Article 1: Land belongs to the nation and every Mauritanian, without discrimination of any kind, can own land, in conformity with the law.
>
> Article 7: Collective lawsuits concerning property are legally inadmissible. Such lawsuits now pending before the courts and tribunals will be struck off the rolls by special decisions of the jurisdictions concerned. The decisions or judgments to strike such lawsuits off the rolls are not appealable.
>
> Article 9: Dead lands are the property of the state. Land which has never been developed or whose development has left no trace is considered dead.

---

[10]Christian Santoir, "Le Conflit Mauritano-Senegalais: La Genese," *Les Cahiers des Sciences Humaines d'ORSTOM*, Serie B, May 1991.

Traditional tenure rights were undermined by Article 7, which made it impossible for any traditional claims to be enforced through the courts. What is particularly problematic, however, is the part of this Article that prohibits any access to court to challenge decisions: this is a clear violation of the right to a fair trial, set forth in Article 14.1 and 16 of the International Convenant on Civil and Political Rights. The provision in Article 9, whereby registered land title takes automatic precedence over traditional rights, reinforced the bias against those with customary land rights only.

Article 21 of decree 84.009, supplementary to the original decree, required that "Any collectivity that wishes to retain lands undivided must transform itself into a regularly constituted cooperative in which the members have equal rights and duties." Since traditional tenure was founded upon precisely inequality of rights and duties between the notables and others, this was an obstacle to black communities taking advantage of this provision. Although as stated above, Human Rights Watch/Africa does not take a position in disputes about title and use of land, the practical effect of this requirement is to deny access to land to those who had held it for generations. In practice, local beydane authorities were given the power to confiscate traditional black lands with impunity.

On the face of it, the law itself was not racist; its application, however, was altogether different. Subsequent decrees and circulars relating to the law's application -- Decree 84–009 of January 19, 1984, Circular 0005 of April 14, 1984, and Circular 007 and 0020 of July 29, 1985 -- were issued by the Minister of the Interior and gave the local authorities broad powers to deal with the land questions as they saw fit.

The law should have affected the whole country, but in reality, it was applied only to the land in the south belonging to the blacks. Had the law been applied uniformly throughout the country, beydane land-owners who farmed the fertile oases of the north would have been adversely affected, as explained by Samba, a former Mauritanian teacher:

> The text of the law is perfect, but the application makes it undeclared apartheid. If the law was just and fair, they would have expropriated Moor lands in the north that are worked by haratines. Instead, they had to find the cover of law, and that's why they initiated the land reform.[11]

The selective application of the law was also described by Boubacar, an

[11]Interview in Dakar, Senegal, March 6, 1991.

exile in Senegal:

> We learned from the radio that land had become national property. At the same time, the radio said that the government would use its discretion to allow a certain part to be cultivated by former owners, but the rest, always according to its discretion, was now national. We knew that land in the north is untouchable...Therefore the announcements on the radio about land reform were mystifying to us - if land in the country had been nationalized, why in practice did this seem to affect only our land -- the land belonging to blacks? It's clear that everything was happening from the perspective of the dam. Obviously, the government had told beydane businessmen that they could acquire the land in the south. This is the only motive behind the 1983 reform. It had nothing to do with the government's desire to make land a national domain as such.[12]

According to the law, land that did not show signs of being exploited -with such indications as irrigation ditches and marks of cultivation -- could be expropriated by the state. Article 2 of Decree 84.009 states: "To be legally protected, the development of a plot must include constructions, crops, or dikes for retaining water."

This provision failed to take into account a number of factors that would have helped secure lands owned by blacks. First, the combination of the drought and the severe economic crisis in the country had deprived black farmers of the means to cultivate all their land. This was aggravated by the fact that they were effectively barred from receiving bank loans or credits that could have enhanced their production. SONADER (the French acronym for the National Corporation for Rural Development) and the banks,[13] apparently only supported projects in the south that would be run by beydanes. Blacks could rarely secure any loans for projects in the river valley; the loans that they were able to obtain were for insignificant amounts. The banks hiring practices reinforced the discrimination against loans for blacks: Bank officials were all Moors, with the few blacks relegated to administrative positions. Second, the

---

[12]Interview in Dagana, Senegal, June 1990.

[13]In 1988, the two principal banks -- the International Bank of Mauritania (BIMA) and the Mauritanian Banking Corporation (SMB) -- merged to form the National Bank of Mauritania. Others were branches of banks based in the Arab countries.

requirement that fields show traces of irrigation ditches to avoid being declared "dead" ignores the local agricultural methods. As explained above, cultivation patterns are based on the annual floods, and many fields cannot be cultivated every year. Constructed irrigation ditches are rarely used.

The land reform also established procedures for granting concessions based on the number of hectares involved. Article 22 stipulated that concessions from five to thirty hectares had to be approved by the Minister of Finance; more than thirty hectares required the approval of the Council of Ministers. These procedures were seen as unnecessarily cumbersome by many members of the beydane community, who pressured the government to simplify the procedure. The government responded by creating a major loophole in the legislation, to the benefit of the beydanes, as follows. In the subsequent circulars of application, "temporary" land concessions were granted, which bypassed the established process of approval. Concessions that were not considered "major investments" were exempt from the procedures for approving registration detailed in the 1983 law, and could be approved by local authorities. According to Park:

> The operative word is *major* ("importants" in the original text), which allows circumvention of the legislation where local authorities do not feel the concessions are of truly significant size. This rather large breach in the legislation was clearly designed to facilitate the new strategy of developing the Senegal River Basin under the aegis of, and for the profit of, Bidan [beydane] entrepreneurs.[14]

Just as the blacks were being dispossessed of land, many high-level officials and their relatives obtained large plots of land at the time that the land reform went into effect. A Mauritanian sociologist gave this account: "More than half the land in the Trarza region is owned by fifty-six people, all of whom have between 100 and 600 hectares. Of these fifty-six, fifty-five are Moors, one is black."[15]

METHODS USED TO EXPROPRIATE BLACKS' LANDS

Several methods were used to expropriate blacks' lands, all of which violated the due process rights of those affected. Some of the means described in detail on the following pages exploited the provisions of the land reform, and

---

[14]The Park study, p. 16.

[15]Interview in Dakar, Senegal, March 4, 1991.

others either bypassed the requirements of the reform or ignored them altogether. Perhaps the most common method was confiscation through registration. Blacks were prevented from establishing or enforcing their legal claims to land, which were instead allotted to beydanes who were able to use their influence in the bureaucracy to obtain documents for land registration. A second method was the establishment of fake cooperatives, whereby beydanes would become members of previously black cooperatives, and sometimes take over the cooperatives altogether. This allowed beydanes to penetrate registered landholdings. Often, there was blatant disregard for the legal requirements set forth in the land reform. A final method was the violent expulsion of black farmers in 1989–90, and the subsequent "indirect expulsions."

Corruption among local and national officials plays an important role in facilitating expropriation of land belonging to blacks. Some regional governors or local prefects take the land for themselves, their friends, or members of their tribe; others help to settle Moors on black lands in order to advance the Arabization of the country.

Confiscation Through Registration

The most common method used to seize blacks' land proceeded as follows: northern beydanes with access to bank loans and credits usually denied to blacks, would approach authorities in the south about acquiring plots of land. These authorities would then declare the black-owned land "dead" (*terres mortes*), in accordance with the 1983 law, claiming that there were no signs of cultivation. Arguing that the proposal did not involve "major investments," the local authority authorized a "temporary" concession, and the land was registered and leased to the new owner.

The land reform established certain procedures to be followed before land could be confiscated. In theory, the characteristics of the plot in question were to be explained in detail, including its location and geographic attributes. The proposed transfer of ownership was to be announced on the radio and posted at the local governor's or prefect's office. Anyone who had claims to the plot in question were to present themselves to the authorities within one month. If no one challenged the transfer, it went into effect.

As with so many laws in Mauritania, the regulations of the land legislation were applied in a discriminatory fashion. In addition to violating the due process rights of individuals, these practices amounted to *de facto* but official discrimination against the black ethnic groups, in violation of Article 26 of the

International Convenant on Civil and Political Rights.[16] First, the radio announcements and posters at the governor's office were usually in Arabic, and sometimes in French. Most black landholders did not understand Arabic, although many do understand French, and the announcements were never made in their native languages -- Pulaar, Soninké, or Wolof. (Predictably, the text of the land reform was not available in the native languages either.) In addition, the governor's office in many regions was far away from the blacks' villages, where they would be unlikely to see a posting about their land. In any case, many black farmers were illiterate. The local authorities often delayed announcing a proposed land acquisition until days before the deadline, making it effectively impossible to mount a challenge.

The most important factor in confiscation through registration was the complicity between the beydane businessmen, who wanted the land, and the local authorities, who wanted them to have it. Also important was most black farmers' lack of land title documents, a fact that was used and manipulated by the beydane authorities. Often, the authorities demanded land title documents from black farmers. The minority who could produce them were safe -- for a while; the others would be vulnerable to immediate confiscation. One of the "lucky" ones was Abdul, a farmer who was forcibly expelled in 1989 and gave Human Rights Watch/Africa the following account of his encounter with the authorities:

> Around [late 1983], I had other problems with [one] plot of land, a garden. Half of it I had used to cultivate dates and the other half to cultivate sweet potatoes. The district supervisor came and wanted to know "if all this belonged only to me." When I said yes, he replied that it was too much for one person. He gave half of it to a beydane. I told him he had no right to do this. He said that I should come the next day to his office with the relevant title deed. If I did not do this, he stated that he would simply take the land and give it to someone else. The next day, I took the papers to his office. The title deed I had was itself older than the district supervisor himself. As soon as I gave him the papers, he said I could go; all he needed

[16]Article 26 states: "All persons are equal before the law and are entitled without any discrimination to the equal protection of the law. In this respect, the law shall prohibit any discrimination and guarantee to all persons equal and effective protection against discrimination on any ground such as race, color, sex, language, religion, political or other opinion, national or social origin, property, birth or other status."

> was the papers themselves. I was able to harvest normally between 1984 and 1989. But before I could gather the 1989 harvest, I was deported in June.[17]

Human Rights Watch/Africa learned that, soon after the 1983 land reform was issued, prominent blacks tried to get their communities to legalize their rights to land. Beydane officials often frustrated this process. Boubacar (quoted above) explained the difficulties he faced when, after the district supervisor, accompanied by armed guards, visited his farm and threatened him, he requested legal title to the land:

> As expected, they refused. I persisted with the request. I saw three prefects in succession, as each left to be replaced by another one. The last prefect I saw in Rosso was black, Demba Sarr. He called the district supervisor and asked him why he had not given the land to me [i.e., registered it in Boubacar's name]. The Moor district supervisor replied that they wanted to see "if the land really belonged to him. If he gave in easily, the land is not his, but if he persisted -- with the risks implied -- then it is because it is really his."

Boubacar went on to describe how Sarr angered the central authorities by refusing to accept their reasoning and was eventually transferred and replaced by a beydane. Boubacar also explained how his repeated efforts to secure title to his land continued even after the district supervisor and head of the gendarmes came to tell them to stop farming the land. He said:

> We all refused to stop and we continued to work the land up to harvest time. We harvested, we sowed the tomatoes. They came back and told us again to stop. We told them we could not afford to stop because we were financed by banks, and if we didn't pay our debts, we would go to prison. Therefore, we had to work to reimburse our debts. Shortly after that, we were deported.[18]

In the absence of registration documents, confiscation was much more straightforward. Human Rights Watch/Africa was told about numerous cases,

---

[17]Interview in Dagana, Senegal, March 2, 1991.

[18]Interview in Dagana, Senegal, June 1990.

of which the following is one example:

> In 1988 in Bababé, a Moor from the north went to the local prefect and said he wanted some land. The prefect told him to choose what he wanted, and then sent out a communiqué describing the land, as the laws required. The seventy-year-old man whose land was in question presented himself to challenge the acquisition. He was told to show his papers proving the land was his, which he could not do. He lost the land.[19]

In theory, the smaller land concessions were supposed to be temporary, but they quickly took on a permanent character and have since become indistinguishable from the larger confiscations.

Establishment of Fake Cooperatives

Another method of expropriation involves the establishment of fake cooperatives. According to the law, traditional collectivities may register large areas of land for cultivation as cooperatives -- a system that in theory allows for the adaptation of traditional forms of landholding with little change (subject to reservations noted earlier). As a result, many of the registered black-owned lands were registered as cooperatives.

Confiscation of registered land required a strategy different from that used for unregistered land: penetrating the cooperatives and ultimately taking them over. The testimony of Abou Bakary, quoted below, includes an example in which half the membership of an all-black cooperative was replaced by beydanes, on the instructions of the authorities. Finally, all the blacks in the village were expelled, and the entire cooperative was taken over by beydanes.

Alternatively, authorities could force blacks to form cooperatives with the beydanes, the beydanes being the *de facto* landowners, and the blacks the laborers. The entities that resulted from this process were cooperative in name only, in fact being vehicles for exploitation and land confiscation. Abdul, in Dagana (Senegal), explained how he was forced in 1983 to form a cooperative to farm four plots of land. Thirty of the cooperatives' forty members were beydanes, including its new president. He went on to describe how half the land was then expropriated, as follows:

---

[19]Interview in N'Dioum, Senegal, March 1, 1991.

> I received a proposal that I should establish a cooperative with a group of beydanes who had no land. Normally, a cooperative has forty people. In this instance, thirty members of the cooperative were beydanes who did not own any land. In addition, the local authorities insisted that the president of the cooperative be a beydane and I, the proprietor of the land in question, became a mere member. The land being "managed" by this cooperative belonged only to me. The other nine blacks who packed the cooperative did not own any land either. The land was enormous and was used to cultivate millet. Once the cooperative was set up, all the other members paid a contribution and exploited the land.
>
> One day, the district supervisor came, accompanied by a beydane, and told me that from now on, half of this land belonged to the beydane. We continued to exploit the land under the new system, that is, the half that now belonged to us. Even the other beydanes did not complain openly about this decision because the beydane in question, a member of the Isselmou tribe, was supported by the district supervisor and was therefore more powerful. This happened in early 1989. Between 1983 and 1989, I resigned myself to the situation that was imposed on us. There was no choice. The thirty beydanes who were from the north represented other powerful beydane interests, such as businessmen, etc. The thirty beydanes did not all live in the village.[20]

ENFORCEMENT OF CONFISCATIONS

Blacks who have tried to resist the expropriation of their land have felt the full force of state-sponsored repression. Villages that tried to save their land quickly encountered the wrath of the state. Abdoulaye, from Monga, a village to west of Beylane, explained how such resistance led to his arrest and torture:

> The Moors who were given my land told me not to cultivate it. The law says that if there are signs of cultivation, they can't take it from you -- that's why the Moor forbade me from cultivating the land. I went to see the district supervisor, the prefect and the governor -- I

[20] Interview in Dagana, Senegal, March 2, 1991.

> even wrote to the Ministers of Rural Development and of the Interior. Because of this, I was locked up for a week at the gendarmerie in Bogué in December 1988. I was severely mistreated there -- I was beaten, subjected to "jaguar" (see chapter on "The Massacre of 1990-91") and tied up.[21]

Abou Bakary Thioun, a religious leader from Jow Reo in the Brakna region, told Human Rights Watch/Africa how he and other villagers were abused after a conflict with beydanes. Ever since the land reform went into effect in 1983, the authorities had been interested in the land owned by his village. In 1988, as he described, they became aggressive:

> In June or July 1988, just before the harvest, about one hundred beydane civilians came to the village and insisted that the villagers split the harvest with them. When the village refused, the beydanes came back -- this time, with guns and gendarmes. A violent confrontation ensued, which left several blacks and beydanes wounded. The local authorities were called in and arrested eighty-six blacks and twenty beydanes, all of whom were taken to Bogué.
>
> During investigation at the National Guard Camp in Bogué, the treatment of the blacks and the beydanes was markedly different: the blacks were split up, severely mistreated and some were held for two months; the beydanes were released almost immediately. We were called in one by one and told to accept that the land belongs to the state, that we blacks had no right to monopolize the land. If we didn't accept, we were beaten. After three days, all but fifteen of us were released, but seven were re-arrested the following day. We were then sent to Aleg prison, where a new investigation began. We were denied visits from lawyers and families, and were given just enough food to survive. Finally, two months later, we were allowed to return to our village.

Shortly thereafter, the district leader came to announce the new land distribution. He said:

> Out of one hundred members of the cooperative, fifty were banned,

---

[21]Interview in Beylane, Senegal, March 1, 1991.

> replaced by fifty beydanes -- including the twenty who had been arrested. I was still in the cooperative; about half of the blacks who had been arrested were kicked out. The beydanes didn't have to pay for the land, and the blacks who were thrown out of the cooperative received no compensation. In fact, we all had to pay the state 30,000 ougias (150,000 CFA) and, twenty days after our return, all the rice harvest was confiscated. The rest of the land in our village that was not being cultivated was given to the beydanes. After the land was given to the beydanes, if you spoke against it, you would be arrested for a few days.[22]

Deportation completed the process a few months later: In June 1989, the National Guard came, surrounded the village and forced everyone to cross the river to Senegal -- some one hundred families, comprising about 600 people.

A similar situation took place in the village of Gourel Moussa in 1988. The village chief, Mamedou Alia Djigo, tried to resist the government's decision to confiscate the village's land. His opposition led to his arrest and imprisonment. In 1989, he and the entire village were deported to Senegal.[23]

When villagers tried to seek legal redress for the confiscation of their land, they found that the same authorities who sold their land to the beydane businessmen were also capable of controlling the judiciary. A Mauritanian who had worked for the Ministry of Rural Development described one such case that occurred in 1986 in Fanaye Niakwar, in Trarza, where an international organization was involved in a development project. The governor, Mohamed Lemine Salem Ould Dah, in conjunction with the former secretary general of the Interior Ministry, Fall Oumar, stopped the project and arrested some villagers for not informing them about the project. Fall Oumar took the materials that the NGO had brought to the village -- motorpumps and other machinery -- to his own village, Taiba. The land in Fanaye Niakwar was given over to a beydane businessman. The villagers tried to take the matter to court:

> The villagers got together and hired a lawyer -- a white Moor, since a black lawyer had no chance of success. The lawyer made an official request with the court of Rosso, but got no response from the president of the court. In fact, the court never responded officially,

---

[22]Interview in N'Dioum, Senegal, March 2, 1991.

[23]Africa Watch telephone interview from New York, June 3, 1992.

although the president told the lawyer privately that the case couldn't be resolved by the court because the state wouldn't allow him to deal with it as a legal matter. The villagers tried everything -- they wrote to the minister of the interior, the minister of justice, even the President of the Republic. The entire matter remained blocked until 1989, when all the villagers were deported.[24]

Continuing Abuses Since 1989

In 1989, the conflict over the land in the Senegal River Valley took a new turn involving unprecedented violence and human rights abuses. This was the episode of the mass expulsions of black Mauritanian citizens, described in the Forcible Expulsions chapter of this report. In addition to attempting to alter the ethnic-demographic and political structure of the country, and to enact retribution for the abuses against Mauritanians in Senegal, one of the principal aims of the expulsions was to accelerate the seizure of land from black farmers. Many of the white Moors are considered by the government to be "displaced" persons, i.e., refugees from Senegal, whom the government has sought to install in the abandoned black villages.

In the period since the mass deportations of mid-1989, the pressure on black farmers has remained constant. Forcible expulsions have continued, albeit at a slower rate, and the military occupation of the Mauritanian side of the valley has provided the context for many abuses against the black population there, including land confiscations. The government has also armed many of the Moor populations along the valley. Continuing abuses against the black population are described in the chapter on the military occupation of the Senegal River Valley.

[24]Africa Watch telephone interview from New York, June 1, 1992.

5
MASSACRE OF 1990-91

From November 1990 through February 1991, 500–600 black political prisoners were executed or tortured to death by government forces. The victims were among the approximately 3,000 blacks arrested between October 1990 and mid-January 1991,[1] allegedly because they were involved in an attempt to overthrow the government. The prisoners, most of whom were from the military and some of whom were civilians, were held in incommunicado detention and subjected to extreme torture, apparently in an effort to extract confessions and information about others.

Reports about the deaths were first heard in late March 1991, after political prisoners who were released in an amnesty revealed the fate of the hundreds of their fellow detainees who had been murdered and tortured. Many who survived were reportedly crippled, paralyzed, or maimed from the torture, and some are believed to have died after their release as a result of the lingering effects of the torture. Almost all the deaths involved black members of the military, and all belong to the Halpulaar ethnic group.

Despite abundant evidence directly linking high-ranking government officials to human rights abuses against the black ethnic groups, the Mauritanian government refuses to acknowledge responsibility for these deaths and injuries or to allow any independent investigation. In order to guarantee immunity for those responsible and to block any attempts at accountability for past abuses, an amnesty was declared in June 1993 covering all crimes committed by the armed forces and security forces between April 1989 and April 1992.

THE ARRESTS

The arrests took place throughout the country, but centered on Nouakchott, Nouadhibou, and Aleg. The government initially targeted blacks in the military, but later expanded their focus to members of the civil service. Some of those arrested were released without charge after days or weeks in detention; others were charged with treason, but no trial ever took place. Among those arrested were members of Mauritania's small navy, customs officials, members of the

---

[1]Amnesty International, in its April 5, 1991, press release, claims that 3,000 were arrested. The U.S. Department of State, in its annual *Country Reports on Human Rights Practices for 1991*, states that there were "possibly as many as 3,000" arrests. Some Mauritanian exiles believe that the number was as high as 5,000.

army, police officers, civil servants and even ordinary civilians.

The arrests resulted in what one Mauritanian refugee termed "a psychosis of fear" among the blacks, caused not only by the huge numbers being arrested, but also by the apparent arbitrariness of the process. A black Mauritanian who was in Nouakchott at the time of the arrests described the atmosphere:

> During the arrests, there weren't any blacks who felt safe. Since many of the arrests took place in the middle of the night, people often went to bed with their clothes on. My cousin was arrested in his pajamas -- he didn't even have shoes on. When you left the house, everyone knew that if you didn't come back, you had been arrested.[2]

The Mauritanian government justified the arrests with the charge that Senegal had backed the alleged coup attempt, which Senegal denied. However, this justification is implausible for several reasons: First, the charges were announced only in December, even though the arrests began in October. Second, black soldiers would have been unlikely to attempt a coup after the dramatic decrease in the number of black army officers and soldiers following the alleged coup attempt of October 1987; most of those who remained in the military were disarmed.[3]

The arrests may have been related to an electoral campaign for mayor of Nouakchott, which was being contested by Messaoud Ould Boukheir, who was galvanizing the black and haratine populations against the government. Accordingly to this logic, the government would have fabricated the coup attempt in order to show Mauritanian society that the blacks were dangerous. If this was in fact the government's reasoning, it was unnecessarily extreme: most blacks were not able to obtain either new or updated identity cards, which were required for voting.[4]

---

[2]Telephone interview from New York, May 2, 1991.

[3]Many blacks from the army, the police force, the National Guard, the various security services and the customs service had been expelled in 1989 and 1990.

[4]According to some unofficial estimates, only fifteen to twenty percent of the population voted in the mayoral election. The low turnout was due in part to the ineligibility of blacks to vote, and in part, to their lack of faith that the election would be free and fair. As one Mauritanian told Human Rights Watch/Africa in a telephone

A refugee interviewed in Dakar on February 18, 1991, took a more sinister view of the arrests:

> We weren't surprised by the arrests in 1990; it is part of a policy to exterminate the black Mauritanians. In order to get rid of the blacks, those in the military and in the civil service had to be arrested. It was especially important to get the blacks out of the military, because that's the only institution that could take power.

One of the black officers, a brigade commander at a military school, expressed the bewilderment of many others when he described his arrest on December 6, 1990, in Atar:

> On Thursday morning, they began arresting blacks in Atar. The security officer, Mohamed Ould Gafar, came with his gun and said, "Lieutenant you must respond to the company commander." The commander, Cpt. Cheibatta, made me sit and said he had received a message from Nouakchott to arrest me. I was astonished -- what did I do, did I break some regulation? I was shocked. He said he didn't know anything. The Commander of the Military School -- Abderrehim Ould Sidi Ali -- received an order from Nouakchott that ordered the captain to arrest: Cpt. Bâ Pathe, Lt. Diagana Chouaibou, Lt. Diop Hameth, Lt. Abderrahmane Mamadou Dia, Lt. Diaw Djibril, Lt. Soumare Mamadou, Sous-Lt. Diagana Abdoulaye Youssouf, Sous-Lt. N'iang Ibrahima, MSgt. Diallo, Sgt.Maj. Dembele, Sergeant Sow, MSgt. Bousso.
>
> They held us for four days -- from the 6th to the 10th -- in back rooms and humiliated us. They barely gave us any food or drink. We were guarded by armed soldiers -- Moors. At that point, we weren't tied up. They just took our epaulets and all our belongings.
>
> On the 10th, we were taken in Buffalo air transport planes -- they blindfolded us, tied our hands -- they didn't want us to know our destination. We didn't know anything -- what we had done, where

---

interview from New York on May 2, 1991: "I wouldn't call these elections; they were a pretense of elections."

> we were going, if we were going to die.[5]

A Chief Warrant Officer interviewed by Human Rights Watch/Africa was arrested on November 27, 1990 and taken to Inal. He gave the following account of the mistreatment and, in some cases, executions, to which he and his companions were subjected upon their arrival:

> They took me to a room where I found soldiers with guns, as well as a warrant officer of one of the companies. They told me to take off my clothes, which I did. They made me lie down and tied my hands and feet behind. I had only my underwear on. Then they blindfolded me and took me to another room. There I heard some noise. I asked who was there and found out that some friends of mine were there: Sy Mbaye, Bâ Mamadou Samba, and others.
>
> We stayed there until the middle of the night. Then they made us board a truck, and took us to Inal. Inal is 400 kilometers away from the base. We arrived around 4 A.M. Throughout all that, we were tied, with our feet behind us. Sometimes they would beat us. They urinated on us. They walked on us and would say just anything they wanted. They said: "You will see that you will no longer exist. We will kill all the blacks, all the black Africans."
>
> When we arrived in Inal, at 7 A.M., we saw people lying down. We thought that they were people who had been beaten up, but they were dead bodies.[6]

CONDITIONS OF IMPRISONMENT

Because the great number of arrests necessitated expanding the government's capacity to house detainees, unofficial detention centers came into use: Military bases and police stations in various parts of the country were transformed into internment camps, and buildings around the capital were turned into prisons. Reports indicate that the detainees were held in buildings belonging to the army, the National Guard and the police in Nouakchott and Nouadhibou, and in military bases in Aleg, Neima, Rosso, and Foumgleta.

---

[5]Interview in Paris, France, November 10, 1991.

[6]Anonymous interview in Nouakchott, Mauritania, September 1991.

One of the main detention centers was the military barracks at Jereida, about thirty kilometers north of Nouakchott.

In late March 1991, Cheikh Fall, a black company warrant officer in the army who was stationed at Jereida, sought political asylum in France and released his story to the French press.[7] According to Fall, the authorities began to use Jereida as an internment center in November 1990.[8]

At Jereida, the officers were split up and put in two kinds of cells: 90-by-90 cm. and 180-by-180 cm. The smaller cells held about four men; the larger cells held ten to fourteen men. In both types of cells, there was not enough room for everyone to lie down. There were no windows, only slots through which the food was passed. According to Fall, thirty-two officers and about 286 noncommissioned officers were detained at Jereida. Fall himself was arrested for three days, from December 9–12, and was released after the intervention of some Moor friends. He returned to Jereida after his release, where he witnessed the following scene of abuse and execution:

> All the black detainees were tied up. The soldiers were put in rooms, dormitories, with guards in front. The building for the clinic was also guarded.
>
> The black detainees came in sealed trucks. They were in terrible shape. Sometimes they came from far away -- undressed, arms tied behind their backs, feet tied. Some came blindfolded. Some even had cotton sponges in their ears so they couldn't hear. Some hadn't eaten for two or three days. Some were wounded from torture. Some even died during the transport -- there were at least three, an officer and two soldiers. The officer was Oumar N'Dao N'Diaye; he was an army lieutenant who worked in Akjoujt.[9]

One of the officers interviewed by Human Rights Watch/Africa described his arrival at Jereida and the conditions of detention. He called the following

---

[7]Stephen Smith, "L'Apartheid est Maure," *Libération*, (Paris), April 5, 1991.

[8]Interview from New York, April 30, 1991, and in Paris, November 1991.

[9]Interview in Paris, France, November 10, 1991.

account of mistreatment, forced labor and lack of hygiene the first phase at Jereida.

> Things really began when we were getting out of the trucks: they called our names one by one -- it's terrible to recount -- and they'd hit you and accuse you of being a *Flamist* [members of FLAM]. At that point, we began to realize that the arrests were political. "You'll die here," they said, "dirty blacks -- foreigners in this country." And to see soldiers hitting officers!
>
> The noncommissioned officers were put in a hanger. People from Nouakchott were already there, and had been there since November. The noncommissioned officers were used as forced labor to build a mosque in Jereida.
>
> The conditions of hygiene were awful. We ate so as not to die, but sometimes there was sand and shells in the food. You had to urinate in the cell; they often wouldn't give you permission to go to the bathroom. From 6 p.m. until 7 A.M., they usually wouldn't let you leave the cell. So we tried to reserve a corner of the cell for the bathroom. Sometimes we were allowed to go outside, but always guarded. When our comrades became sick, we tried to give them something that they could get sick into.[10]

TORTURE

In all the detention centers, most of the detainees were savagely tortured in an effort to extract confessions and information about others. The prisoners were told to sign a confession -- without having the right to read it - that acknowledged their participation in a clandestine military organization set up to overthrow the government. An officer named Diagana explained the process to Human Rights Watch/Africa.

> The detainees were put in the hot sun, and one by one they would be brought before the commission. They would ask questions -- if you say you didn't know why you were there, you'd be taken out and

---

[10]Interview in Paris, France, November 1991.

> tortured. If you didn't want to be tortured, you had to lie and say you knew about the coup.[11]

As Fall explained, the torture was often performed in the courtyard of the barracks. "It wasn't done discreetly. The detainees could hear the cries," he said. Fall went on to describe the horrific torture of one of the detainees:

> I saw many cases of torture. A Lieutenant Baal, in December, for one. He was a pilot in the air force. I knew him for years. When I saw someone sleeping -- I didn't even recognize him. They had beaten him for fifteen minutes with rubber tubing and stripped him naked. He had his arms spread and attached, also his legs. A cord was attached to his neck. They beat him on his chest and his genitals. There was blood flowing from his mouth. He screamed. Finally he said he was part of the coup and had arms hidden at his home. They walked on him and threatened to rape his wife. The torture lasted more than two hours. They said, "You give us names of other officers with you." Then they sent a message to the army to check his house for arms -- but they found no arms or anything at all. So they called him back. They began to beat him but realized that there was no point. He signed a confession.[12]

The torture of detainees was so relentless that confessions were often obtained. As Diagana told Human Rights Watch/Africa: "If you signed, there would be no more torture. You were put in other cells designated for those who had finished. In the end, everyone signed."

Information gathered by Human Rights Watch/Africa identified the following torture methods:

- Beatings all over the prisoners' bodies, using fists, boots, sticks, rubber tubing, electrical cords, rifle butts;

- Stripping the prisoners naked and pouring cold water over them (especially when they first arrived in December, when it was cold);

---

[11]Interview, November 10, 1991, Paris, France.

[12]Interview with Cheikh Fall, November 10, 1991, Paris, France.

- Burying the prisoners in sand up to their necks. While they were buried, soldiers would pull their hair out, and burn their faces with lit cigarettes. Fall saw a soldier named N'Daraw N'Diaye die this way in December.

- "Jaguar" -- the detainees would be hung over an iron bar, with their hands and feet tied together, and would be turned on the bar and beaten. Water would be thrown on them, and they would be subjected to more beatings.

- A variation on "jaguar" was the use of an iron bar, like one used for doing pull-ups. The detainees arms would be attached to the bar, so their feet could not touch the ground. They would hang like that for hours, until their shoulders were extremely painful and sometimes internal hemorrhaging would occur.

- Burning all over the body, including the bottoms of the detainees' feet, with fire.

- False executions -- late at night, black officers would be taken about five kilometers from the barracks, blindfolded and informed that they were about to be executed, before being taken back to the camp.

- Burning, electric shock and beating of genitals.[13] There were also reports of castrations.

Diagana explained that he was beaten for three days, December 22-25, but refused to comply with their demands that he sign a "confession." He provided the following description of his torture:

> The interrogators were officers of military security, including: Lt. Hacen Nagatt; Lt. Samory Ould Youmbaba; Lt. Ely Ould Dah; Lt. Daha Ould Cheikh; Sub Lt. Brahim Ould Bouzouma. First, they beat

[13]In the U.S. State Department's *Country Reports on Human Rights Practices for 1991*, it is reported that at Inal: "some of the detainees were tied by their testicles to the rear of four-wheel-drive vehicles and dragged at high speeds through the desert. Several of the detainees, including Cpt. Lome Abdoulaye, a former senior officer in the Mauritanian navy, died as a result of this particular treatment."

> us with electric cables and said "you are *Flamists* [members of FLAM], we have proof, if you don't confess, we will make you." I said no, I was never part of any organization, I don't get involved in politics. Then they tortured me with "jaguar." They beat me; they tied me so tight that I still have scars. I was tied up, naked, and beaten on my back. They beat me until I was almost unconscious and tried to record everything I said during the beatings. When you regained full consciousness, they said "speak or we'll start again." Most people said fine -- I'm a *Flamist* -- they'd say anything to avoid more torture. Me, I said no -- I'd rather die. I never said I'm a *Flamist* and they had no proof whatsoever. So I was subjected to three days of beatings -- from December 22-25. They beat me everywhere -- all over my body, including my genitals. I thought I would be sterile.
>
> In my confession, I said that I don't belong to any political organization but that my colleagues and I did speak about the problems of advancement in the army. For five years -- since 1986 - no blacks had been admitted to Officer training courses, which you need to pass to the rank of Captain. They want to eliminate blacks from the army. I took the test three times and never passed. On December 25, they finally accepted this as my confession.
>
> The soldiers and the noncommissioned officers were not allowed to read what they signed. But it said: "I address this confession to you. I was contacted by such or such officer, and I am part of a clandestine military organization that's mission is to organize a coup d'etat."[14]

Alassane, a thirty-year-old black soldier, fled from Mauritania to Senegal in April 1991. In an interview in a hospital in N'dioum,[15] he described beatings, chainings, being buried in the sand, and other abuses as part of his detention:

---

[14]Interview in Paris, France, November 10, 1991.

[15]Interview in N'dioum by a foreign worker and a Mauritanian refugee, April 13, 1991.

> We were imprisoned first in Aslat for a while, then we were transferred to Haym, and then to Nema, where we were held in a building....My life in prison was filled with constant torture, beatings, hands tied behind my back, and feet chained. It was often in this position that the beatings would pour down on us. They came without warning, when prisoners were sitting down or doing nothing. I don't think there was anything they didn't do to us....
>
> At the beginning, when they arrested us in Aleg, they tied our feet and hands, then they dragged us through the thorns and over the hot sand. In my case, for example, I was buried in sand up to my neck while two people hit me in the face and threw sand at my face. Others were subjected to the same treatment; some even died as a result. That's how Niokkane died.

A military doctor arrested on November 24, 1990, interviewed by Human Rights Watch/Africa, described his detention in Inal, and the difference in treatment meted out to the commissioned and non-commissioned officers:

> The commander of the Nouadhibou region -- Sid'Ahmed Ould Boilïl -- called me, saying I was needed. He said I had been denounced by others who had been arrested. I was never political. I was a soldier. I did what I was supposed to do and then went home.
>
> I wasn't allowed to make any phone calls. I was taken to the base, told to undress and was blindfolded. They tied me up tightly -- and put me in a room. I screamed, so they loosened the ties slightly. Then I was taken to the north, about 250 km. from Nouadhibou, to Inal. Others who had already been arrested were there -- they were all from the military, and all Pulaars. There were about twenty of them.
>
> The officers were pretty much left alone after they confessed, but the noncommissioned officers -- they would cry and cry and cry during the beatings. It was horrible hearing them scream. Many of them died. There were 180 deaths at Inal.[16]

---

[16]Africa Watch telephone interview from New York, July 8, 1991.

The Chief Warrant Officer interviewed in Nouakchott was also detained at Inal. He gave the following account of savage torture and hangings he encountered on his first day in Inal:

> At 9 A.M., the Captain of the base of Inal came with two groups of six people, each with a whip. They began to beat us, and did so from 9 to 11:30 A.M.
>
> Afterwards they took us to a warehouse where we found friends of ours who were almost dead, people who couldn't even talk. The place was stinking, as if there were only dead bodies there. They then tied us with chains which were there and beat us every hour and insulted us, dirty words. They said we are savages who shouldn't have existed, that we are people who cannot be in Mauritania. They said that all the blacks should no longer exist in Mauritania; that we were in their hands and that they were going to kill us one by one and afterwards kill all the remaining population, that they were going to kill all the adults and only the children would be left, and these children would be taught Hassaniya or Arabic. French, Pulaar, Soninké, and Wolof would no longer exist in Mauritania.
>
> They kept on torturing us until around 7:00 P.M. The first person I saw hanged in front of my eyes was a soldier called Idi Seck. They took the rope, put it around his neck and tied him. They left him till he died. It was the first person I saw hanged.
>
> Afterwards, around midnight, they brought ropes, made three rows of ten people each and hanged thirty people. It was on the occasion of the feast of November 28 [Independence Day].

Another officer interviewed by Human Rights Watch/Africa was detained at Inal from December 13 to January 11. He described a number of torture techniques that were used, unsuccessfully, to make him confess to being part of FLAM:

> On Thursday, December 13 at 1:00 in the afternoon, I was at my brother's house. He had been arrested on October 27, and was also a gendarme. I went to visit his family to see how they were doing.

> A brigade commander and four gendarmes surrounded the house; they arrested me and took me to the gendarmerie. I found three other officers there -- one captain and two lieutenants. They undressed me and put me in a WC -- for twenty-nine days. The WC was about 1.5 meters square. I was not able to sleep -- it was cold and I was nude, and they threw cold water on me every night. They beat me -I lost a tooth. In the morning, they would give me a bit of bread, and a little to drink.
>
> They accused me of being a member of FLAM, and said that I was an agent for FLAM during 1988–90, when I was in France for medical care and to visit my family. I refused to sign anything, even though they tried to make me sign.
>
> Each day there was mistreatment. They put water in my right ear, then sand. They were interrogating me. This happened two times -- on December 15 and 17. At about 4:00 in the morning, you would hear people crying, so you knew something was happening. That's when they would come to beat you.
>
> On January 11, they freed me. I was required to stay home, and I was watched.[17]

DEATHS IN DETENTION

The severity of the torture, combined with the complete lack of medical care, ensured a high death toll. At this writing, the government still refuses to acknowledge the deaths, and no accurate statistics are available. However, the figure of between 500–600 deaths from torture or summary execution is widely accepted.

Cheikh Fall was responsible for registering the detainees at Jereida; according to his figures, there were 424 detainees in February 1991. Fall estimates that some thirty blacks died as a result of torture at Jereida. The victims' families were never notified; the bodies were buried in scattered places three or four kilometers from the base. According to Fall:

> People usually died after [the torture]. You could barely recognize them. Many died in the clinic -- there were no medicines for them,

---

[17]Interview from Paris, November 12, 1991.

and no doctors. There were two nurses there, but basically the detainees were put in the clinic so that they wouldn't die in front of their comrades.[18]

The following are a few cases of those who were tortured to death:

- Ly Moussa, a man in his late forties, from Dar el Barka in the department of Bogué. For many years, he had worked as a businessman in Nouadhibou, principally as a fish exporter. In 1986, he was arrested and accused of being part of FLAM. He was sent to the infamous Walata prison, where he and the other political prisoners were subjected to torture and gross mistreatment. After four of the prisoners died in 1988, conditions improved somewhat, and they were transferred to Aioun prison. He was freed in December 1989, and returned to his family and his business in Nouadhibou. In November 1990, he was arrested again, related to the alleged coup attempt. He died in detention.

- Kane Abdrahmane, a meteorologist in his early forties from Tekane, near Rosso. For his last fifteen years, he lived in Nouadhibou and worked for the Association for the Security of Aerial Navigation (ASCNA). He was arrested in November 1990 in Nouadhibou.

- Sow Ibrahima, an army sergeant in his early thirties from Medina Fanaye in the Trarza department. During the Sahara War, he fought for Mauritania, was taken prisoner by Polisario, and finally released in 1981. He lived in Nouakchott with his two wives and three or four children. He was never involved in politics. He was arrested in November 1990.

- Ball Souleye, an army corporal in his early thirties, originally from Medina Fanaye in the Trarza department, although his family lives in Rosso. His father, Ball Alhousseinou, was killed by security forces during the expulsions of 1989. Ball was serving in Aleg, where he was arrested in late September or early October.

[18]Interview in Paris, November 1991.

- Sal Oumer, a marine lieutenant in his early forties, from Niakwar, in the Department of Trarza. He was a religious man who was not involved in politics, and lived in Nouadhibou with his wife and five children. He was arrested in November. He died on November 28. A witness stated that "his mutilated body was indescribable."

- Dia Ousmane, an officer, died in the night in early January 1991 after being tortured. His hands were tied behind his back, he was stripped naked, and he was put on the ground and beaten with whips. About five soldiers were involved, each beat him until he got tired, and then the next would take over. This kept going until the prisoner said "Stop -- I'll talk." Then they poured cold water over him. He began to shiver -- it was cold during January. He died a few minutes later. A few soldiers were designated to bury him.

- About thirty detainees died at Jereida, and are buried about five km. north of the barracks. Among the dead are: Chief Warrant Officer Guisset Mamadou, Company Warrant Officer Ly Mamoudou and Colonel Aw Oumar.

- In December, Sub-Lt. Dia Abderrehmane died after he was beaten savagely. He was from the village of Djingue.

- Captain Lome, from the navy, was strangled and beaten all over his body. He died on November 26-27.

The day of his arrest, Alassane witnessed the beating deaths of six other detainees. He said:

> They died from being beaten. The guards took one and began to beat him with truncheons, and he screamed "I wasn't a part of it, I wasn't a part of it" until he finally died.... One of them was named Ball, from the Toro area. Another's name was Niokkaane, from somewhere near Kaedi. Another was Sergeant Diop, also from someplace near Kaedi. Another's name was Niang, from Garalol.

In addition to those who died as a result of torture, an unknown number of blacks were extrajudicially executed by the security forces. Although information on such cases remains sparse, Human Rights Watch/Africa has received details about the following executions of black detainees.

- In the camp at Jereida, four soldiers and one sergeant -- Dia Abdoulaye, Sow Abdoulaye, Sy Moussa, Garly N'Diaye, and Sy Hamadi Ali -- were forced to dig a grave in which they were buried, after they were executed.

- At Inal barracks, north of Nouadhibou, twenty-eight soldiers were hanged on November 28, 1990. Reports indicate that the executions were performed in honor of Mauritania's Independence Day.

THE GOVERNMENT RESPONSE

Ample evidence points to the direct involvement of many high-ranking government officials. In its *Country Reports on Human Rights Practices for 1991*, the U.S. State Department asserts:

> It appears that the highest levels of the military hierarchy -- including several members of the CMSN [Military Committee for National Salvation] -- were involved and may personally have taken part in torture or execution.

Despite the magnitude of evidence, the government has not acknowledged the killings, and has repeatedly refused to permit an independent commission of inquiry to investigate the deaths, allowing only a military commission whose findings were never made public. No one has been charged or tried in connection with the torture and massacre.

Nabil Bouaïta, a French lawyer who has tried to represent the widows of the massacre victims in suits against the government, described his difficulties with the Mauritanian authorities:

> So as not to be accused of being manipulated or tricked, the collective [an international collective of lawyers which he represented] tried to consult the Mauritanian authorities. The Minister of Justice, after having confirmed our meeting, canceled it without explanation the very hour that it was due to be held. This hardly conciliatory attitude shows the inconveniences of dealing with the cold indifference with which the victims of all abuses are treated.

> During my visit to Mauritania, I discovered that a veritable wall of silence has been constructed around this subject and that the attempts to identify those responsible are failing....[19]

A serious blow to hopes for prosecuting those responsible for the deaths occurred in December 1991, when two colonels,[20] both CSMN members, who were directly implicated in orchestrating the massacre, were promoted. The two men, Col. Sid'Ahmed Ould Boilïl and Col. Cheikh Ould Mohamed Saleh, were the commanders of the military regions of Nouadhibou and Aleg, respectively, where most of the killing and torture took place. Both men had effectively been put on six-month probation before their promotions. The timing of these promotions was particularly surprising, given that Mauritania was seeking international support for its first democratic presidential elections in January 1992, and signalled a clear rejection of accountability for human rights abuses. Other officers apparently involved in the massacre were Maj. Mohamed Cheikh Ould El Hadi and Maj. Ely Fall.

In addition, after announcing the pardon for political prisoners in 1991, the government dismissed from the army an unknown number of officers, seventeen of whom wrote a letter of protest. One of them told Human Rights Watch/Africa:

> In mid-March, we were visited by Deputy Chief of Military Staff Col. Sidia Ould Yahya and Capt. of Military Security Ely Vall. They told us that we would be dismissed from the army because they had proof that we belonged to a clandestine anti-national organization. They said that a commission of inquiry would see us. But they had already judged and sentenced us *before* the commission!
>
> The sixteen officers were the last to be released. When the amnesty was announced -- they didn't even tell us, a non-commissioned officer told us. Later, the commander of the base came and confirmed it. I was given forty-five days and then had to present myself to the military headquarters in Nouakchott.

---

[19]Nabil Bouaïta, "Qui a peur de la vérité?", *Jeune Afrique* #1612, (Paris), November 20-26, 1991.

[20]There is no higher rank than colonel in the Mauritanian army. The promotion involved new responsibilities assigned to the two colonels.

> I returned to the military headquarters on June 1, after the forty-five days. From June 1-9, we were considered like military, but they didn't tell us much. We were twenty-seven officers -- eleven from Jereida and sixteen from N'Beika. On June 9, they divided us in two -- ten officers were taken back to the army, and the rest were told that as of a certain date, ranging from twenty-five to sixty days from then, we were no longer members of the military. The older ones, seven of them, were sent into early retirement. The rest were dismissed for disciplinary reasons. For doing what?[21]

In order to guarantee immunity for those responsible and to block any attempts at accountability for past abuses, an amnesty was declared in June 1993 covering all crimes committed by the armed forces and security forces between April 1989 and April 1992. It is no coincidence that this period corresponds to the height of the abuses against Mauritania's blacks, including the massacre of 1990-91.

PUBLIC PROTESTS OVER DEATHS

In a rare show of public opposition to the government, a series of open letters and tracts have been issued in Mauritania criticizing the government's role in the arrests and killings. Human Rights Watch/Africa has received the texts of some of these documents, written by groups of intellectuals, workers, and women. They provide important and often moving testimony to the efforts of Mauritanian citizens to hold their government accountable for these abuses.

Intellectuals' Letter

On April 10, 1991, fifty prominent Mauritanians -- including former ministers, lawyers, doctors, and professors -- signed an open letter addressed to President Taya that denounced "the magnitude of the repression that was brought down upon the blacks civilians and military in the last months of 1990." Among the abuses, they listed several hundred extrajudicial executions, atrocities, and disappearances. The letter linked the abuses to broader government policies, as follows:

> Such violations of the rights of men and citizens are likely to reinforce a climate of suspicion, of defiance and of permanent tension

[21]Interview in Paris, France, November 1991.

> which will prevent the cohesion and stability of our country. These violations are also a harsh shock to the noble ideals of Islam, especially religious tolerance, brotherhood and the respect of the human being. It is for these reasons that these violations constitute a dangerous and unique precedent in the history of our country....
>
> These tragic and regrettable events are the logical consequence of a policy of blind repression that makes no distinction between the guilty and the innocent. They are even more the result of the absence of democratic freedoms.

The letter called on the government to form an independent commission of inquiry to determine responsibility for the crimes and to take immediate steps to guarantee the rule of law.

Workers' Declaration

On April 18, 1991, the Mauritanian Workers Union (UTM -- Union des Travailleurs de Mauritanie) published a statement calling for a national conference to discuss democraticization and for an independent inquiry into the 1990 detentions.

Women's Petition

Also in April 1991, more than seventy-five women -- wives, sisters, nieces, and mothers of some of those presumed to have been killed in the detentions -- signed a petition addressed to President Taya. The women called on the president to break the official silence surrounding the deaths and to help provide for the families left behind. They wrote:

> The disappearance of our loved ones presents immeasurable problems on many levels, especially socially. Some of these men were the only sons, and were therefore the only joy and pride of their families; others provided the only means of support; and others still left behind several wives and many children without resources.
>
> With the crumbling of our last hopes, we are living in a true tragedy. We have the bitter feeling that we are being left alone with our grief and its surrounding misery. We have been put in a situation that human conscience cannot accept.

> For these reasons, we appeal to you as a last recourse so that the silence will be broken, that explanations will be given, and that humane treatment will be accorded us...

This petition was followed in mid-May by the announcement of a Solidarity Committee. Their statement, signed by 363 women, declared:

> For the past several weeks, the conscience of our people has been deeply troubled by the testimonies and revelations of a number of the victims of these last arrests -- these real "survivors of the death camps."
>
> If the President was right when he stated that not one more political prisoner remains in prison today, then those prisoners who stayed in the camps might be there forever.
>
> Accordingly, hundreds of brave sons of this nation are dead, not "in the service of their country," but rather, somehow "devoured by their own army."
>
> Faced with this drama, seventy-five women -- mothers, widows and sisters of the victims -- wrote an open letter on behalf of their families to the head of state. They asked that official notification be given to the affected families, so that the religious and social obligations can be observed.
>
> Such a request naturally demands the formation of an independent commission of inquiry in order to find those responsible, identify the guilty, and prosecute and punish them in accordance with the law....
>
> All the valiant and legitimate efforts by our sisters have encountered a wall of silence from the authorities....
>
> This is why, faced with this situation, we, the undersigned Mauritanian women, have decided to establish a committee of solidarity with the families of the disappeared....

On June 11, 1991, a group of women held a demonstration in Nouakchott calling for the government to release information about their relatives. The demonstration was broken up by police, who reportedly kicked and beat the women, at least ten of whom were hospitalized.

The Widows

The women's petition signaled the start of the mobilization of widows into a significant force demanding accountability for human rights abuses in Mauritania. The widows have undertaken various actions designed to pressure the government to acknowledge the massacre of 1990-91 and to prosecute those responsible. Using a combination of public statements and efforts at legal redress, the widows have also attracted international attention, and sent representatives to the United Nation's Conference on Human Rights, held in Vienna in June 1993.

As part of the government's campaign to ensure impunity, which culminated in the amnesty of June 1993, the government has sought to buy off the widows. In early 1993, the government apparently contacted more than 200 of the widows around the country and offered them their husbands' pensions. The widows responded by organizing a series of meetings with their counterparts throughout the country -- including in Bogué, Rosso, Kaedi, Djoel, and Bababé -- to sensitize them about the dangers of accepting the government's money without any official information about their husbands' deaths, leading to the prosecution of those responsible. According to one of the widows, only two women accepted the government's offer -- and in both cases, it was because the woman's father forced them to take it.[22]

One group of widows, known as the Collective of Widows of the Victims of Repression in Mauritania, published a statement in a September 1993 issue of *Le Calame*, an independent newspaper. The statements condemned the June 1993 amnesty, calling it "unjust and in flagrant contradiction to the constitution and the laws in practice in Mauritania."[23] The widows repeated their principal demands, which include: that pensions be given to the families of all those killed; that the Collective of Lawyers be permitted to represent the widows and seek civil damages for all the victims; that the amnesty of June 1993 be repealed; that an independent commission of inquiry be formed to establish responsibility for the killings. The widows also called on human rights organizations, religious groups, and political parties to join with them in

---

[22]Interview in Ourosogui, District of Matam, Senegal, October 30, 1993.

[23]Collectif des Veuves des Victimes de la Répression en Mauritanie, "Déclaration," *Le Calame*, #9, (Nouahchott), September 13-19, 1993.

pursuing the rule of law in Mauritania.

In fact, a Collective of Lawyers was formed to represent some 188 families of the victims in demanding prosecution of those responsible for the massacre. Members of the collective have been subjected to harassment and intimidation by the government, including the following incidents: One of the lawyers, Diabira Maroufa, was detained and threatened in 1991; attacks were launched against the Collective in the government press; the Ministry of Justice refused to accept the collective's letters; and the Minister of Finance demanded that additional taxes were owed by members of the collective. According to a letter written by Diabira Maroufa on December 3, 1993, "the government's objective is to force the members of the Collective to renounce their demands for justice by threatening their [professional] survival."

6
SLAVERY

On July 5, 1980, the government of president Mohamed Khouna Ould Haidallah passed a decree abolishing slavery. It was the third time in Mauritania's history that slavery had been banned.[1] In November 1981, the government issued an ordinance encouraging judicial authorities to enforce the provisions of the 1980 Decree. The ordinance declared that "slavery is definitely abolished throughout the national territory" and added that former slaves hold all the rights previously denied to them. However, the abolition was essentially a public-relations exercise prompted by external considerations.

The institution of slavery continues today in Mauritania, especially in the countryside. Tens of thousands of blacks are considered the property of their masters and are subjected entirely to their masters' will. They work long hours for no remuneration. They are denied access to education and do not enjoy the freedom to marry or to associate freely with other blacks. They escape servitude, not by exercising their "legal" rights, but mainly through escape. Ignorance of their rights, fear of recapture and the torture that often follows, and the lack of marketable skills in an impoverished country discourage a substantial number of slaves from trying to escape. Slavery is said to be particularly widespread in the eastern part of the country.

Human Rights Watch/Africa recognizes that abolishing slavery, which is deeply rooted in Mauritania, is a difficult and long-term process. However, the persistence of slavery is largely due to a lack of will by the authorities to end the practice. Successive governments have not taken steps to fulfil the important responsibilities Mauritania undertook when it passed laws and ratified international conventions prohibiting slavery. Slavery exists today because legislative enactments have not been accompanied by necessary initiatives in the economic and social field.

Seeking to convey the impression that slavery is a problem of the past, government literature refers only to "haratines," or freed slaves. In the cities, the Arabic term for slave, *abd*, has been abandoned in favor of "the blue ones" (*les bleus*) or the "Sudanese" (*les Sudanais*). Other terms for slaves include "pupil" or "domestic" -- domestics who are not paid, have no rights and are entirely at the mercy of their employer.

---

[1]Slavery was abolished for the first time in Mauritania by the French in 1905, and again under the 1961 constitution.

However, such changes mean little to the slaves themselves. A recently escaped slave told Human Rights Watch/Africa:

> Of course slavery still exists today in Mauritania. The reason is simple. Whatever emancipations there have been, we continue to work for the same master, we continue to do the same kind of work for no pay and to live under the same conditions. Nothing has changed, except in words. We have not been given either the education or the economic means to become aware of our rights and to take advantage of them. The worst is the countryside, where most of the slaves live. There, it is ancient Mauritania; slaves don't even know they have rights, and they don't know anything about emancipation. I had heard of the abolition, but it had no practical effect on my life.[2]

Human Rights Watch/Africa, which has repeatedly been denied permission to visit Mauritania, is not in a position to confirm the number of slaves. In 1981, after a visit to Mauritania, the London-based Anti-Slavery Society calculated that "...the country probably holds a minimum of 100,000 total slaves with a further 300,000 part-slaves and ex-slaves."[3]

A huge number of slaves fled the countryside for the cities between 1969 and 1978, prior to the Anti-Slavery Society visit. Two major events facilitated their departure. The first was the severe drought of 1969–74 which led to hundreds of thousands of Mauritanians, including many slaveholders, coming to the towns in search of better economic opportunities; many slaveholders who remained in the countryside sent their slaves to work in the cities and the mines near Zouerate. The second event was the 1975–78 war over the Western Sahara for which there were massive recruitment drives. Because no comparable events have occurred since 1981, the estimates given by the Anti-Slavery Society may still be basically accurate.

MAURITANIA'S LEGAL OBLIGATIONS TO END SLAVERY

Slavery is expressly prohibited by international law and by a number of international treaties to which Mauritania is a party. Article 4 of the 1948

---

[2] Interview in Senegal, June 1, 1990.

[3] John Mercer, *Slavery in Mauritania Today*, London: Anti-Slavery Society, 1982, p.1.

Universal Declaration of Human Rights specifically outlaws slavery as follows; "No one shall be held in slavery or servitude; slavery and the slave trade shall be prohibited in all their forms." Several other articles of the Declaration prohibit the characteristic features of slavery, such as the denial of freedom, of dignity, and of equal protection before the law. Other articles protect many of the fundamental rights which slaves, by definition, do not enjoy, such as the right to freedom of movement, the unfettered right to marry and found a family and the right to remuneration for work.

Five other conventions ratified by Mauritania address the question of slavery.

- The 1951 Convention for the Suppression of the Traffic in Persons and of the Exploitation of the Prostitution of Others, ratified on June 6, 1986;
- The 1957 Supplementary Convention on the Abolition of Slavery, the Slave Trade, and Institutions and Practices Similar to Slavery, also ratified on June 6, 1986;
- The 1930 Forced Labor Convention of the International Labor Organization (ILO);
- The 1957 Abolition of Forced Labor Convention of the ILO;
- The 1981 African Charter on Human and Peoples' Rights, which affirms individual equality before the law and rights to liberty, property, and equal pay for equal work, while prohibiting the domination of one people by another.

In its annual report released in 1993, the ILO denounced the continuing problem of slavery in Mauritania.[4]

THE HISTORICAL ROOTS OF SLAVERY

Slavery has existed in Mauritania for many centuries. Blacks were brought north after capture by raiding Arab/Berber (beydane) tribes. The possession of slaves was considered a symbol of the status of the individual and the tribe, but

[4]Stanley Meisler, "U.N. Agency Assails Sudan, Mauritania on Slavery," *The Los Angeles Times*, March 9, 1993.

economic considerations were also attached. The slave who lived and travelled with the nomadic household looked after the needs of the family. Traditional sources of income, such as animal husbandry and agriculture, relied on slave labor.

Slaves were not permitted to marry, and their children belonged to their masters. The power of slaveholders over their slaves was absolute: slaves could be killed by their masters with impunity. Even when they were killed for insignificant reasons, which happened frequently, their murders were ignored by the authorities.

Haratines, whose children did not belong to the former master, had the legal right to own property and enter into contracts. Traditionally, haratines became emancipated through several different routes. One route was through the French colonial army. The French sought recruits for the army among both the blacks living in the south, and the beydanes who preferred to "contribute" a slave instead of being recruited themselves. Those slaves were later emancipated. Most of the educated haratines are the sons and grandsons of slaves who were "given" to the French colonial army. Other haratines became free after finding jobs and labor purchasing freedom for themselves and their family. Haratines have kept the language and customs of the beydanes.

By the turn of the century, France was the administering power in Mauritania, and in 1905, France adopted a decree abolishing slavery. It was abolished again in the 1961 constitution, which guaranteed all citizens equality before the law without distinction of race, religion, or social status. Neither measure succeeded in putting an end to the system because no practical measures were taken to enforce the abolition. The inadequacy of the provisions was underlined by the fact that haratines who tried to exercise their new-found freedom were returned to their masters by local authorities, including magistrates and policemen, many of whom owned slaves themselves and regarded the abolition as a threat to their self-interest. Prior to 1980 and since then, slaves became emancipated usually by purchasing their own freedom, or more commonly, through escape.

THE EL HOR MOVEMENT

In 1974, haratines founded El Hor, derived from the Arabic word meaning "the free," as a pressure group to advance the interests of their community. Hoping to raise consciousness among the slave and haratine communities, El Hor distributed tracts and organized demonstrations. The group argued that emancipation was impossible without practical measures to enforce anti-slavery laws and provide former slaves with the means to gain economic independence.

To this end, it called for land reform and encouraged haratines to set up agricultural cooperatives.

El Hor became involved with a controversial case involving the sale of a slave woman, Mbarka, in Atar in February 1980. There was nothing uncommon about sales of slaves per se. What distinguished this case was that an educated haratine, Lt. Barak Ould Barek, wanted to marry the slave in question. As she was considered particularly beautiful, her master decided he could sell her for a great deal of money on the open market. At the marketplace, two beydanes wanted to buy her and the case came to attract national attention, and served as the vehicle for releasing pent-up expressions of broader grievances. El Hor organized demonstrations in Nouakchott, Rosso, Nouadhibou, and other towns.

El Hor's emphasis on social issues and its demands for redress and justice inevitably brought it into confrontation with the government. Frightened about the possible consequences of El Hor's activities, the government's initial strategy was repression. The authorities clamped down with particular ferocity. A substantial number of the movement's leaders and members were arrested, severely tortured, and many of them exiled in 1979–1980, signalling the government's unwillingness to allow the existence of an independent forum agitating for the rights of haratines.

In January 1980, a military coup brought President Haidallah to power. The new government took a number of steps to undermine the movement by appearing to satisfy its demands. The steps included the "abolition" of slavery on July 5, 1980. The proclamation was also prompted by President Haidallah's desire to forestall any possible political links between the opposition, led by former president Moktar Ould Daddah, and black opposition groups. Other steps included co-opting some of El Hor's spokesmen by granting them high government posts, promotions, and economic opportunities.

El Hor was at its strongest in 1978–1982; it still exists today.

SLAVERY IN MAURITANIA TODAY

The persistence of slavery in Mauritania is due largely to inadequate efforts by the government to educate slaves regarding their rights and to punish slaveholders for continuing to own slaves. The prevalence of slavery is demonstrated by the fact that even haratines in high government positions often have brothers and sisters working in the house of a master. In an interview with Human Rights Watch/Africa, Moustapha, a shepherd who escaped from his master in March 1990, discussed the lack of information available to slaves:

> I never heard the abolition discussed in my master's house. I learned of it from some Halpulaar villagers living near us. I don't know of any slave who got to know about the abolition in his master's home. All the ones I have met who have heard of it learned from other black communities, which is why masters are so sensitive to any contact between slaves on the one hand, and free haratines and other blacks, on the other hand.

He went on to discuss the repercussions of seeking out those who would explain his rights:

> If the master suspects that you are visiting free blacks, severe punishments await you. The first time I heard of the abolition, I was indifferent because I did not believe it. Then I began thinking about it and I became more curious. I returned to the same Halpulaar neighbors to seek an explanation. My master became suspicious when I came back late and he found out that I had seen our Halpulaar neighbors. In order to show his displeasure, I was undressed, my hands and feet tied up and I was made to lie flat on my stomach in the burning sun. I was then whipped with a whip made of cowhide and during the night, when the temperature was cold, they kept pouring cold water all over my body.[5]

Traditionally, slaves have no right to marry or found a family. Children born to a slave woman are the property of her master; slave parents do not have any rights to their children. Moustapha told Human Rights Watch/Africa about the sale of a slave child:

> Slaves are still bought and sold. The last sale I remember happened during the last winter season [November 1989 to February 1990] when a boy of two was sold by his master, Mohamed ould Mbarak to Naji ould Rouej. The mother had just stopped suckling the boy. The sale took place in a village called Drajni in the region of Trarza.

Slave couples living in the cities may enjoy a degree of family life, such as a tent to themselves, but in the countryside, there are no formalities

---

[5]Interview in Senegal, June 1, 1990.

governing marriage. Usually, when two slaves "marry," the masters make the necessary arrangements. Even if the woman is allowed to join her husband's household, her original master may call her back to his house at any time; the wishes of the masters always take precedence over those of the slaves.

The Buying and Selling of Slaves

The government argues that the sale of slaves ended in the 1960s, but the extensive interviews conducted by Human Rights Watch/Africa contradict these claims. While the public sale of slaves in the open market has disappeared, former slaves told Human Rights Watch/Africa that in the countryside, the system has merely been refined and disguised. Frequently, the slave himself is not aware what kind of agreement has been reached.

Diop, a black health worker who was married to a haratine, described some of the methods used instead of an open market:

> Slaves are still bought and sold but with a difference, that is without the publicity that was previously considered so distasteful. Nowadays, beydane tribes make discreet arrangements among themselves. A slave is given in exchange for something else. Then there are the "presents." I recall the case of a young woman who had a child. The child, who was eight months, was given to a cousin of the master, as a "present" for life. It was agreed not to transfer the child to his new owner until the mother had stopped breast-feeding him.[6]

Several independent sources reported a 1983 case in which a black officer in the military police was transferred to Boghe after he protested the sale of a slave at the market in Boutilimit.

The case of a fourteen-year-old slave girl, Salkha Bint m'Bareck, gained attention in October 1992. She was given to her master in partial payment for a car, but pretended she was sick. When she was taken to Nouakchott, she escaped to a cousin's house, and they went to the police to complain. According to her cousin, Marietou Said Sayyid: "The next day, they arrested her and called her master."[7] El Hor hired a lawyer to defend Salkha, but the courts

---

[6]Interview in Senegal, May-June 1990.

[7]Quoted in Michelle Faul,"Slavery Abolished in Mauritania, but Continues Nonetheless," *Associated Press*, April 4, 1992.

sent her back to her master on the grounds that she was a minor and there was no one else with responsibility for her.

Religion

Religion, as manipulated by masters, has been important in the perpetuation of slavery. Slaveholders have used Islam's recognition of slavery to justify current practices. However, Islam recognizes slavery to the extent that non-Islamic captives caught after holy wars may be treated as slaves, on condition that they are released upon their conversion to Islam. In Mauritania, people living as slaves were all Muslims long before the first abolition in 1905, but they were not emancipated. Human Rights Watch/Africa received numerous complaints about the extent to which qadis (judges in Islamic courts) continue to exercise their judicial functions to protect the institution of slavery, rather than to ensure its eradication.

All those who spoke with Human Rights Watch/Africa about slavery emphasized the extent to which slaves are conditioned, both by their masters and religious leaders, to regard serving their masters as a religious duty. Human Rights Watch/Africa was told of many local expressions used to teach slaves to accept their subordinate position as a condition for going to heaven. Mawliid, fluent in Hassaniya, was a student at the University of Nouakchott. His family had lived in various towns in the north. He said that the phrase, "the way to heaven is underneath the sole of your master's foot" is commonly used to sum up the attitude towards slaves and religion.

A religious leader from Aleg elaborated on the religious dependence of slaves on their masters:

> It is difficult for a slave to go to the mosque to pray because they have not been taught what to recite. After the last abolition, the masters intimidated their slaves by telling them that their choice was to follow them or to go to hell. Given the culture they had lived in all their lives, it is easy to understand why so many believe this.[8]

Education

Unlike haratines, slaves do not have opportunities to attend modern schools. Some slave children are permitted to attend Koranic schools (religious

[8]Interview in Senegal, May-June 1990.

schools) but such a privilege is entirely at the discretion of the household.

A number of black religious leaders interviewed by Human Rights Watch/Africa said that they never had a slave as a pupil in their Koranic schools. The following was a typical comment:

> I never had a slave as a student in Koranic school. They are not permitted to attend. I only had as pupils a few whose parents had escaped to the city; otherwise, no slaves came as students. Once at school, if they are regarded as having developed a "disrespectful" attitude, they are sent to the countryside to tend the animals.[9]

All the former slaves who spoke with Human Rights Watch/Africa saw education and training as the basic tools for emancipation, including Bilal, a haratine, who is a fisherman from Nouakchott.

> If slaves are ever going to be free, education is their most fundamental weapon. The master knows this too -- that is why he resists educating his slaves. He knows this will eventually lead to freedom. In order to maintain their servitude, if there is any possibility that the slave is having contact with free blacks, the master promptly dispatches him to the bush.

The Economy of Slavery

Nowhere is the failure to confront the reality of slavery more apparent than in the economic field. A former slave, a butcher working in a village along the Senegal River Valley, summarized the total economic dependency of slaves in the following terms:

> There is physical slavery and there is economic slavery. Even though physical slavery has been abolished, nothing has been done about economic slavery which is the best way to guarantee both physical and psychological slavery.

Abdoulaye, a black Mauritanian who grew up in the North, is a former government employee who had previously worked in a private enterprise. He explained that former slaveholders often obstruct the path of former slaves

---

[9]Interview in Senegal, May-June 1990.

seeking financial independence:

> No economic measures were adopted to help former slaves -- none. On the contrary, many masters did everything in their power to prevent their slaves from obtaining jobs and therefore a measure of economic independence. In the first place, haratines have severe problems finding work, and when they get a job, they are constantly intimidated by their former masters. A few years ago, I was working in a private company. I had hired two former slaves. Their former master came to see me and said that these were his former slaves and he regarded their current attitude towards him "disrespectful"; therefore, I should fire them. I refused. From that moment on, I had problems at work because of him.[10]

The specter of unemployment looms before slaves who contemplate leaving their masters. They have not had any training and have nowhere to go. The authorities have done nothing to prepare the community for the economic and psychological dislocation that would confront slaves who try to exercise their new rights. The well-educated haratines who have succeeded financially, or have been appointed to senior government posts, are the exception to the rule of unemployment and poverty suffered by many former slaves. The senior government positions of haratines were regarded cynically by those interviewed by Human Rights Watch/Africa, who saw the appointments as window-dressing by the government. In 1981, John Mercer, who visited Mauritania for the Anti-Slavery Society, wrote:

> The hartani [haratine] has trouble finding employment: the men only get the worst jobs, such as rubbish disposal in its various forms, the women will sell cooked couscous, perhaps even open tiny restaurants, often drift into prostitution.[11]

Human Rights Watch/Africa's research corroborates Mercer's findings. The pre-existing difficulties have been exacerbated by the drought that devastated Mauritania in the early seventies and forced hundreds of thousands of people to come to Nouakchott, Nouadhibou, and other cities, competing for

---

[10]Interview in Senegal, May-June 1990.

[11] Mercer, *Slavery in Mauritania Today*, p. 8.

employment. (The drought is estimated to have killed 75 percent of the country's livestock.)

Embarrassed by the publicity generated by the report of the Anti-Slavery Society and by a 1982 BBC film that discussed slavery in Mauritania, the government invited the United Nations to send an investigative mission to Mauritania. The visit took place in January 1984 and was led by Marc Bossuyt, a member of the Sub-Commission on Prevention of Discrimination and Protection of Minorities. Peter Davies, then Director of the Anti-Slavery Society, accompanied the team. Bossuyt submitted his report to the Sub-Commission in July 1984.

Among other suggestions, Bossuyt recommended that the government give loans to former slaves to purchase livestock, that it facilitate financial assistance for small enterprises and that it establish new schools, especially in the agricultural sector where most slaves live. In a separate report, Peter Davies highlighted the need for land reform, and for educating the overwhelmingly illiterate slave population; he also recommended a number of practical steps, such as creating a new system of labor.

In 1987, a final report was issued by the Sub-Commission to assess the action taken by United Nations bodies and the Mauritanian government to implement the 1984 recommendations. In its reply, the government stated that it had already implemented the necessary land reform measures in 1983. This claim is disingenuous: As explained in the chapter on Land, the land reform of June 1983 had nothing to do with assisting former slaves and they have not been the beneficiaries. Slaves are given a part of the harvest as subsistence, but only enough to survive on. The haratines who spoke to Mercer and later to the UN team looked to land reform as an essential key to their emancipation; they are still waiting for that reform.

The Psychology of Slavery

Most former slaves and haratines, as well as other blacks familiar with the life of slaves, stressed that most beydanes have difficulty conceiving of blacks as being more than slaves. Tokossel, a secondary-school student at Kaedi, explained that the relationships have continued in the younger generation:

> The interdependence is still profound. I remember when I was at boarding school in Kaedi only a few years ago, the haratine students made the tea for the beydane students, did their shopping and ran all their errands. Whenever a black student and a beydane had a fight, often about the demeaning tasks they demanded of the haratines,

> beydane students threatened to bring "their" slave to pay us back. "Their" slave would be any of the haratines at the school.

Blacks also spoke of the dependency felt by former slaves on their former masters. Human Rights Watch/Africa received many accounts of the descendants of haratines who continue to pay a financial tribute to the original master's family, even in cases where the haratine is educated and has become a successful businessman or professional.

An elderly woman, formerly a slave, explained the difficulties involved in altering the psychology of slavery:

> We hear of abolition, but for most slaves it does not mean much. It is hard to ignore what they have been told all their lives, that without their master they cannot survive, that only he can ennoble them, give meaning to their life and lead them to heaven. They believe this; so how can they also believe that they must escape the situation that promises to give them so much?

In an article published in the 1992–1993 journal of the Anti-Slavery Society, Father François Lefort, who lived in Mauritania for many years and headed Caritas-Mauritania, made the following observation about the psychology of slavery:

> The slave lives in perpetual awe of his masters and is not aware of any other way of life. He would often be utterly shocked if he saw his master work or carry a burden. The bond between slave and master is very strong and in many cases, a hartani would spontaneously continue to help and support his former master and would even "lend" him his daughters and sons to work as servants or shepherds.
>
> Slaves never complain and even those who have escaped do not bear grudges against their former masters except when they have been subjected to violence or abuse.[12]

Mauritania's political tensions have exacerbated the practice of successive

[12]François Lefort, "Abolition is not so Easy," *Anti-Slavery Reporter*, 1992–1993.

governments to deepen the divisions of the northern and southern black populations by using haratines and slaves in confrontations with blacks from the south. In February 1966, armed haratines were employed to quell black student riots in Nouakchott. In the clashes in April 1989, slaves and haratines living in the countryside, who have had the least contact with other blacks, were used to kill, wound, and facilitate the expulsion to Senegal of thousands of black Mauritanians. Haratine militas are used to patrol many areas along the Senegal River Valley.

Torture As Punishment

The brutal punishments suffered by slaves are a central theme in any discussion of slavery in Mauritania. Apart from the "routine" punishments -- beatings with a wet cord while naked, denial of food and drink, prolonged exposure to the sun with hands and feet tied together -- there are several unique methods of appalling cruelty. These methods are reserved for "serious" infringements of the master's law, such as disobeying orders, attempting to escape or even the mere suspicion of wanting to escape, being in contact with free blacks, inciting other slaves to escape, and sexual relations with the master's family. These punishments are intended not only to punish the individual, but also to serve as an example to others. A primary objective of these torture techniques is to ensure that the victim is incapable of enjoying normal sexual relations with women. Women are spared these perverse methods of torture, but only because the primary value of the female slave is her reproductive capacity.

One of these methods, administered to men, is the camel treatment. In this method of torture, the slave's legs are tied to the sides of a camel who has deliberately been denied water for up to two weeks. The camel is then taken to drink and as the camel's stomach expands, the slave's legs, thighs and groin, are slowly dislocated. He is tied to the camel for up to four or five days and is subsequently not given any medical treatment. Moustapha told Human Rights Watch/Africa of an incident involving the camel treatment:

> A slave I know suffered the camel treatment in 1988 in Sharat, west of Boghé. His master suspected him of wanting to escape, because they found him on the road when he was not meant to be there. In addition, he was an outspoken young man who tended to reply back to the master and his family and made it clear that he did not like the life of a slave. He was recaptured and put through the camel method. He was 16 at the time. He is still living with the master's

> family but is so handicapped that he is not capable of performing any tasks.

Another punishment is burning coals. The victim is seated flat, with his legs spread out. He is then buried in sand up to his waist, until he cannot move. Coals are placed between his legs and lit, slowly burning the legs, thighs, and genitals of the victim.

A black health worker described brutal treatment meted out to a slave who slept with the master's daughter and who had sought medical care at a hospital in Atar.

> The boy, who was seventeen, had a piece of wire tied tightly around his genitals and the wire was in turn attached, for two days, to a rope. He was then beaten and water poured all over him. I saw him myself. He had become so handicapped that the master could not use him at all; so he "emancipated" him.

7
DISCRIMINATION VIA ARABIZATION: DENIAL OF ASSEMBLY AND ASSOCIATION

The discriminatory effects of government policies related to "Arabization" in Mauritania have had serious consequences for the civil and political rights of the black ethnic groups. Arabization has been used to suppress the black communities' freedom of expression and association, which in turn have been keenly felt in the areas of language, education, employment, and culture. Since the mid-1960s, successive Mauritanian governments have pursued policies designed to favor Arab culture and Arabic speakers[1] to the detriment of the black African population. These policies of *de facto* discrimination have been used to deprive black ethnic groups of academic, cultural, and professional opportunities, and thus to further their marginalization in Mauritanian society. The term *de facto* discrimination indicates that the central government deliberately and systematically discriminates against the black ethnic groups, although the laws themselves are not overtly discriminatory. In the words of a former Mauritanian professor: "[Arabization] is the key to the dispossession of blacks in terms of political power, economic opportunities, and employment possibilities."[2]

FREEDOM OF ASSEMBLY AND ASSOCIATION

For many years, but especially since the crackdown in 1986 (see chapter on "Arrest and Detention of Black Activists"), the government has engaged in *de facto* discrimination against the black ethnic groups. Such policies involve a continual interference with the rights to assembly and association, often resulting in outright prohibition of public and private black gatherings, including naming ceremonies of newborn infants, marriage celebrations, and funerals, as well as performances of theater, dance, and music.

Authorization is officially required for all such gatherings of blacks and Arabs alike, although in practice only the blacks need such permission. Abdoul, a former teacher, explained how the requirement to obtain authorization has no

---

[1]Actually, the Moors speak "Hassaniya," a dialect very close to Arabic. The languages most widely spoken by the black ethnic groups are Pulaar, Soninké, and Wolof, although they generally choose to be educated in French.

[2]Interview in Dakar, Senegal, February 22, 1991.

basis in law:

> In March 1989 at Kaedi, the marriage of a former student of mine was to be celebrated at my home. I was summoned by the police and told that I did not have the required authorization. I replied that I was not aware of the need to seek anyone's permission and that if they wanted to retain this system, such rules needed to be spelled out in writing to enable people to comply with them. Of course there was no law; it was just a practice used against blacks.[3]

These restrictions are used by the authorities in a discriminatory fashion to limit the opportunities for groups of blacks to meet and assembly freely.

In some cases, obtaining the authorization requires traveling long distances, and transportation is often difficult. Meeting the requirements and appearing before the designated authorities does not guarantee that permission to hold a gathering will be granted, which provides further evidence of the discriminatory intent of the government's actions. If an event is held without authorization, the participants risk being interrupted by police; in some instances, the organizers are given a choice between paying a substantial fine or having the police detain all those present. Human Rights Watch/Africa interviewed a number of people who said they had been arrested for failing to obtain authorization. A striking example of the restrictions took place in 1988, when the families of four black political prisoners who died in detention in Walata prison were harassed by police when their friends and families came to pay their condolences (see chapter on "Arrest and Detention of Black Activists"). Tène Youssouf Guèye's widow explained how such harassment compounded the difficulties of the grieving families:

> When people tried to visit us to pay condolences, there were difficulties. The authorities, represented by plainclothes policemen, tried to limit groups by saying that visitors could not stand outside the house. We were fortunate in having a big courtyard inside the house but other families were not so lucky. Djigo Tafsirou's family had no inner court and as it was forbidden for people to congregate outside, the family had to cope with all these additional problems when they

---

[3]Interview in Dakar, Senegal, June 6, 1990.

already had enough difficulties.[4]

In addition to the problems associated with holding such meetings, freedom of association in the cultural sphere has been discouraged by the absence of important black cultural figures, many of whom either were targeted for expulsion or fled the country (see chapter on "Forcible Expulsions"). A Mauritanian economist told Human Rights Watch/Africa about how the suppression of freedom of association and assembly has affected the community:

> For me, the most striking change has been this: all of the Halpulaar's cultural and sporting activities have been suppressed. The artistic and cultural gatherings were where artists or singers would be invited, or where there would be music or theater. Now, it is an atmosphere where things are no longer interesting, so that too is making people want to leave.[5]

The amount of television and radio programming that is allocated to the national languages versus Arabic is indicative of the limits on freedom of expression. In recent years, there has been a steady erosion of the time allocated to non-Arabic languages. The result is that most blacks watch Senegalese television and listen either to Senegalese radio or foreign broadcasts, such as Radio France International, the British Broadcasting Company, and Voice of America.

Some sectors of the black African community attempted to replace the study of both Arabic and French with their national languages, and formed associations for the study of these languages.[6] The government responded to

---

[4]Interview in Dakar, Senegal, May 21, 1990.

[5]Interview in New York, March 27, 1991.

[6]The French language was rejected by many Moors as the language of colonialism. They argued that because Mauritania was an Islamic state, Arabic should replace French as the official language, extending to the educational system. To many in the black communities, the French language, despite its colonial implications, was preferable to Arabic. The blacks, although also Muslim, viewed Arabic as the language of internal domination, and resisted the government's attempts to equate the Muslim religion with the Arabic language. For many blacks, the French language was the only alternative available, since their own languages -- Pulaar, Wolof, Soninké, and Bambara -- were not

these initiatives by suppressing the blacks' rights to freedom of assembly and association. Bellel, who was part of a clandestine organization for the study of Pulaar, was detained in 1974 and again in 1975 about the organization. Even after it was recognized by the government, Bellel said: "[t]he authorities did everything possible to prevent us from propagating our idea." He continued:

> One strategy was to deny us means. For instance, we were denied financial assistance for the use of classrooms to teach literacy classes after 6:00 P.M. when schools had already finished. Even after we collected the money among ourselves, we were refused authorization to rent houses.[7]

The broader issue of discrimination inherent in the language issue was articulated by a Mauritanian intellectual in Senegal:

> Language and cultural problems have plagued this country ever since Mauritania existed as a country. It is not a conflict about languages as such but a question of racism, of skin color. Even if a black is fluent in Arabic, and many are, that does not assure him access to the same opportunities as a beydane or enable him to exercise responsibility even if a black is accorded a senior position in government.[8]

The process of making Arabic the primary language of the country culminated in a new constitution, passed by referendum in July 1991 (see

---

used internationally. French was preferable not only because it was the language in which they had been trained, but it was also the language spoken in many of the countries of West Africa. The blacks' desire to retain French as the official language was rooted in their vision of Mauritania as part of black Africa, rather than the Arab world.

[7]Interview in Senegal, May-June 1990.

[8]Interview in Dakar, Senegal, May 17, 1990.

chapter on "Democratization").[9] Article 6, Section 1, of the constitution states that: "The national languages are Arabic, Pulaar, Soninké, and Wolof; the official language is Arabic." There was no longer any mention of French.

The area of education provides one of the clearest illustrations of the long-term discrimination inherent in the attempts to Arabize Mauritania and the efforts mounted by the black communities to resist it. Since the mid-1960s, the struggle over education has taken on obvious political dimensions.

The Arabization of education in Mauritania may be traced through the various governmental decrees concerning the use of Arabic in the national educational system. The first overtly racial crisis in education took place in January 1966, when a decree was issued stipulating that "Arabic is obligatory for all students entering secondary school as of October 1, 1965." On January 4, 1966, black students in secondary schools in Nouakchott and Rosso went on strike to protest the new requirements, and other sectors of black society called for solidarity with the students. Nineteen black civil servants who supported the students' demands signed "The Manifesto of Nineteen," which detailed a wide range of grievances and condemned what they described as "the total monopoly of all the sectors of national life by Moors." The Manifesto stated:

> This energetic action [by the students' strike] reveals a deep and latent discontent, because it is well known that the compulsory study of Arabic is considered by the blacks to be cultural oppression. This decree constitutes a clear handicap for the black students in their exams; they have consciously turned away from the study of Arabic, which they believe to be against their interest, since it curbs their cultural and scientific development. This is illustrated in the high school of Rosso, where black students who received passing grades in all their courses were left back because they did not pass Arabic.
>
> It may seem surprising that no voices were raised among the black elites and intellectuals to protest a decision that undermines the equality of citizens, especially in an area as important as education.
>
> That is why we, the undersigned, all Mauritanian citizens, declare

---

[9]The referendum took place on July 12, 1991. According to the government, the text was approved by 97.24 percent of the population. However, black opposition activists, including those associated with FLAM, had called for a boycott of the referendum, and they assert that the referendum was passed by a substantially smaller margin.

> our strong and unreserved support for the students' action. We want to begin an immediate re-evaluation of the basis of coexistence between the white and black communities, because we are witnessing the total monopoly of all sectors of national life by Moors.

The signatories were dismissed from their posts, arrested, and some of them tortured. Some subsequently fled to Senegal. (See also chapter on "Arrest and Detention of Black Activists.")

On Feb:uary 6, 1966, black students were assaulted by Moor students, which led to the closing of schools for a short while. Approximately one month later, black students organized revenge attacks on the Moor students. Bloody confrontations that ensued in Nouakchott between the two groups left at least six dead and seventy injured, according to official figures. Unofficial sources estimate that the number was considerably higher. The secondary school students in Nouakchott and Rosso were sent home for the rest of the academic year, and most had to take the year again beginning in the fall.[10]

In 1973, a new provision was introduced, requiring students to study Arabic for two years before beginning their studies in French. After the two-year period, students were permitted to follow a bilingual track, in both French and Arabic.

In 1979, the conflict over Arabic reached a new peak, when a circular was disseminated by the Minister of Education, known as "circulaire 02," which announced two new measures: It increased the subject matter that had to be taught in Arabic by adding a new required class -- Moral, Civil, and Religious Instruction (ICMR) and, most important, it raised the *coefficient*[11] for Arabic in the *baccalauréat* -- the major examination that must be passed to graduate from secondary school. More than any other government action, the circular was seen as a means of preventing blacks from succeeding in the educational system, and the black students went on strike. In the words of a Mauritanian exile in Senegal: "The strike in 1979 marked the point of departure for raising consciousness among the blacks. It showed us that we had to stand up for

---

[10]de Chassey, *Mauritanie: 1990-1975*, p. 393.

[11]Mauritania uses the French system of education, whereby a coefficient is assigned to each subject, and the grade students receive in that subject is multiplied by the number of the coefficient. Accordingly, if the coefficient for Arabic is raised, students across the country who do not speak Arabic as their mother tongue will be penalized and their overall score on the examination will suffer.

ourselves."[12]

The strike prompted the promulgation of a decree that stipulated two important changes: the recognition as national languages of Pulaar, Wolof, and Soninké, and the creation of the Institute for National Languages (ILN).[13] (Bambara, a fourth language that is spoken by fewer people than the other three languages, was not recognized.) The Institute was given a mandate to begin experimental classes in primary schools in the three languages. A former Pulaar teacher who worked at the Institute described the new system:

> The idea was essentially this: if the Moors wanted to teach in Arabic -- their language -- then we wanted to teach in our languages. We weren't against the use of Arabic as one of the national languages, but we opposed it being used as an instrument of oppression.[14]

The experimental classes were to develop a system whereby each child would begin studying in his or her native language, and then would be required to take up Arabic as a second language. (This latter requirement was based on the government's insistence that Arabic should be "the unifying language" of all Mauritanians.) The national languages were supposed to be introduced in October 1986, but instead the government announced that the commission had not finished its work, which would be extended for another year. The black members of the commission protested the decision, to no avail. In the meantime, the arrests in September 1986 of individuals suspected of involvement with the Manifesto of the Oppressed Black Mauritanian included several members of the commission -- Bâ Oumar Moussa, Ibrahima Sall, Djigo Tafsirou, and Samba Thiam (see chapter on "Arrest and Detention of Black Activists"). Members of the institute were also arrested, including Djibril Hamatt Ly, Bâ Aboubaker Kalidou, Mohamed al-Habib Sow, and Toumb M'baye, as well as many of the teachers working in the experimental classes.

The students who had taken the experimental classes fell victim to the decision to discontinue education in the national languages. Since the classes were canceled, the students had to continue their education either in Arabic or in French, and were not allowed to take their examinations in the language in

---

[12]Interview in Dakar, Senegal, February 18, 1991.

[13]Decree 79.348 of December 10, 1979.

[14]Interview in Dakar, Senegal, February 20, 1991.

which they had been educated. According to two former students in Mauritania: "This ensured that the generation of students in the experimental classes would fail."[15]

[15]Interview in Dakar, Senegal, February 1991.

8
ARREST AND DETENTION OF BLACK ACTIVISTS

The security forces in Mauritania include the armed forces, the National Guard, the Gendarmerie (paramilitary police), and the police, which together allow the authorities virtually unlimited power to arbitrarily arrest and detain whomever they choose. Blacks are subject to house searches and arrest without warrants, often on trumped up charges or without any charges or legal basis at all.

Since the publication of a manifesto detailing the grievances of the black community in April 1986 (see below), the government has sought to intimidate the black population into submission. Mass arrests have been a feature of the government's strategy, especially in the latter half of the 1980s and the early 1990s.[1]

In the second half of the 1980s, many leading black activists were rounded up, subjected to farcical trials and then spent years in prison under abysmal conditions. Their imprisonment -- especially at the notorious prison of Walata, but also in Nouakchott and Aioun -- included torture, forced labor, deprivation of food and water, and lack of medical care. Given these conditions, it was not surprising that in 1988, four of the black prisoners died in detention.

LEGAL GUARANTEES

According to Mauritanian law,[2] (Chapter 1, Article 56 of the Code of Penal Procedure), suspects may be held in detention (*garde à vue*) for a period of forty-eight hours. A detention may be extended for another forty-eight hours with the written authorization of the prosecutor or the president of the regional tribunal. In the case of a crime against the security of the state, the period of *garde à vue* may be extended up to a maximum of thirty days, again with written authorization. After thirty days, the detainees must either be released or formally charged.

---

[1]The most egregious example of arbitrary arrest and detention took place in late 1990 and early 1991 (see chapter on "Massacre of 1990-1991"), when up to 3,000 blacks in the military and the civil service were arbitrarily arrested, denied all access to legal counsel or family contact, and subjected to brutal interrogation and torture.

[2]Code de procédure pénale, *Journal Officiel de la République Islamique de Mauritanie*, March 28, 1984, p. 209.

However, the Mauritanian authorities consistently disregard both their own legal procedures as well as internationally recognized rights of prisoners, including the right to due process, access to legal counsel and family visits. Many are held unlawfully beyond the permitted period, and many are held incommunicado.

THE MANIFESTO OF 19

One of the first expressions of black grievances was the "Manifesto of 19," issued in 1966.[3] In the Manifesto, nineteen black civil servants -- teachers, professors, engineers and others -- published a paper criticizing the government's efforts to Arabize the country, and calling for the establishment of a federal system of government.[4] They stated:

> It should be emphasized that at the same time that the Moors express their desire to make Arabic the official language, the black community demands that concrete guarantees be given to prevent all efforts at assimilation, that the national responsibilities be shared and that the constitution be revised into a federal system.

The document went on to reject the Arabic decree and all efforts of cultural oppression, and to denounce the regime's racial discrimination and injustice.

The nineteen were imprisoned without charge or trial for six months in N'beika.[5]

---

[3]Impetus for the Manifesto came from a strike on January 4, 1966, by high school students of the École Normale in Nouakchott, which was followed by a student strike in Rosso. (See also the chapter on "Institutional Discrimination.") The students were protesting the application of a decree that made the study of Arabic compulsory in high schools.

[4]The 19 signatories were: Diop Mamadou Amadou, physics professor; Bâ Ali, computer specialist; Bâ Ibrahima, engineer; Bâ Abdoul Aziz, magistrate; Bâ Tenguella; Sow Abdoulaye, treasury official; Coulibaly Bakary Manso, teacher; Sy Oumar Satigui, teacher; Kane Bouna, history and geography professor; Daffa Bakary, engineer; Bâ Abdoul Ismael; Koïta Fodya; Kane Nalla Oumar, engineer; Bal Mohamed, professor; Traore Jidou, teacher; Traore Djibril, teacher; Sall Abdoulaye, teacher; Bâ Mamadou Nalla, teacher; Seck Demba, teacher.

[5]In the 1970s, some of them went on to hold high-level government positions in the Hadaillah government; at least two now live in exile in Senegal.

THE MANIFESTO OF THE OPPRESSED BLACK MAURITANIAN

In April 1986, the Manifesto of the Oppressed Black Mauritanian (Manifeste du négro-mauritanien opprimé) was published by FLAM. It documented discrimination against Mauritania's black populations in every sector of public life, including politics and the assignment of government posts; the economy; the mass media; the army; and the educational system. The Manifesto described the heightened frustrations of the black communities, and recommended a complete overhaul of the political and social system, as follows:

> Official racism and chauvinism have become daily fare for the blacks. This beydanism or Mauritanian apartheid is practiced on all levels of political, social and cultural life....
>
> The future of the black community in Mauritania will depend on its own solution to this situation. The blacks should only rely on their own will to put an end to the oppression of the beydane system.
>
> We believe that the key to the problem of the blacks and of Mauritania as a whole rests essentially in the destruction of the beydane system and the establishment of a political system that is fair and egalitarian, one with which all the country's components can identify.[6]

In September 1986, thirty to forty black intellectuals were arrested, suspected of involvement with the publication of the Manifesto. Twenty-one were brought to trial, including the following:

Ibrahima Sarr, a television journalist;
Tafsirou Djigo, a former cabinet minister;
Ly Dgibril, an educational administrator;
Tène Youssouf Guèye, a writer and former diplomat;
Ibrahima Sall, a lecturer at the University of Nouakchott;
Seydou Kane, a lecturer and historian;
Amadou Moktar Sow, an engineer;
Abdoulaye Barry, an official in the Ministry of Foreign Affairs;
Samba Thiam, an educational administrator;

---

[6]Reprinted in F.L.A.M., *Livre Blanc sur la Situation des Noirs en Mauritanie*, October 1989.

Idrissa Bâ, a livestock specialist with the Ministry of Agriculture;
Sy Mamadou Youssouf, a treasury official;
Aboubakry Bâ, a teacher and researcher at the Institute of National Languages;
Aboubacry Diallo, a hygiene inspector;
Sy Mamadou Oumar, a businessman;
Gueye Oumar Mamadou, a bank employee;
Sarr Abdoulaye, a professor;
and two sisters -- Piny Sao, a secretary, and Fatimata Mbaye, a law student.

After their arrests, the detainees were subjected to brutal interrogations. Several of them described their experiences to Human Rights Watch/Africa, including Idrissa Bâ, who worked for the Ministry of Agriculture in Nouakchott and was an active trade unionist. He was educated in Arabic and learned French in prison. (He emphasized that speaking Arabic is no protection for a black African in Mauritania.) His family was forcibly expelled in June 1989 and is now living in refugee camps in Senegal. He was arrested on September 8, 1986, after the publication of the Manifesto. Idrissa described the miserable conditions and torture in detention before his "confession":

> During the first day of detention, I was kept in a dark, filthy cell, completely naked. Water covered the cell which made it impossible to sleep. The cell was full of mosquitos.
>
> Then they came and burned a piece of lamb-skin in the cell. The smoke was terrible and the smell unbearable. I was not asked any questions the first day. The next day, I was given my trousers back and told to clear the cell of the water. Throughout, I was always in the hands of Moors. The next day, my hands were tied up with rope and a rope was tied around my neck. I was undressed. They threatened to kill me, there and then, unless I told them who wrote the manifesto and who was responsible for its distribution. I said I didn't know anything about it. I was beaten almost to death by my interrogators, Mohamed and Bush Bush, a Brigadier and Cheiknal, and a policeman.
>
> Between September 8–11, I was given nothing to eat or drink. They prepared a statement and I was told to sign it, if I wanted to eat or drink. I refused. They gave me something to drink but then they beat me and forced me to sign the confession. It was in French. I

did not understand a word of it. During the interrogation I spoke only in Arabic, so they knew I spoke Arabic and not French. Once I had signed my "confession," I was thrown into a big cell with all the other detainees.[7]

Another defendant was Ibrahima Sall, a professor at the University of Nouakchott, who was arrested on September 4. He told Human Rights Watch/Africa about the early stages of his detention:

> At about 8:00 P.M., they took away the blankets; an hour later, they took away the mats, so we had to sleep on the floor. At about 10:00 P.M., they put us all -- Seydou Kane, Sy Mamadou Youssouf and me -- in separate cells. I wasn't allowed to sit down; I had to keep walking. I spent the whole night until 8:00 in the morning just walking around the cell, which measured about two meters-by-two meters. If I stopped, the police threatened me with their machine guns. They didn't give us anything to drink or eat, and we had to urinate in the cell. All the police were haratines. It went like this: all those who interrogated you were white Moors; all those who beat you were haratines.
>
> The next day, I was transferred to a room about two meters-by-three-and-a-half meters with a police guard. I was not allowed to sleep. But the interrogations didn't start until Monday. From September 8-13, I was interrogated by the director of security, Mohamed Ould Dedahi, and two others. The treatment was humiliating -- they wouldn't let you sleep. The whole process was stage-managed.
>
> Since the Manifesto was never signed, we denied our involvement. We were not allowed access to lawyers, and only saw our lawyers on the day of the trial. I finally had to admit that I was a member of FLAM, after they found papers relating to FLAM in my office and later, when they found all the documents relating to the second FLAM congress.[8]

---

[7]Interview with Idrissa Bâ, May 13, 1990, Dakar, Senegal.

[8]Interview with Ibrahima Sall, November 8 and 10. 1991, Paris, France.

On September 24, twenty-one of the detainees were charged with holding unauthorized meetings (Law 73.008 of January 23, 1973), the display and distribution of publications harmful to the national interest (Law 63.109 of June 27, 1963), and making propaganda "of a racial or ethnic character" (Law 66.138 of July 13, 1966). The defendants all pleaded not guilty, but the next day, they were convicted on all counts: Four received six-month prison sentences (Kane, Sow, Barry, Guèye) and seventeen received four and five-year sentences and fines, in addition to five or ten years of internal exile and loss of civil rights.[9]

The trial itself was a farce. Not only were the proceedings conducted in Arabic, though only three of the defendants spoke Arabic, but the defendants were denied access to their lawyers until the day of the trial.

The following account of the trial is taken from testimony by Idrissa Bâ. The detainees were taken to the tribunal at 10:00 A.M. Their lawyers requested a postponement of the trial until September 27 in order to study the files they had just received from the tribunal and to meet their clients, whom they had not been permitted to meet. The tribunal agreed to the request and the defendants were taken back to the prison. But at 11:30 A.M., the detainees were suddenly informed that the trial would begin at 3:00 P.M. the same afternoon. Their lawyers insisted on a postponement. The president of the tribunal refused and the lawyers decided to boycott the trial in protest. (The Mauritanian Bar Association had chosen the defense lawyers who included both beydanes and blacks.) A representative of the government-aligned Mauritanian League of Human Rights was also present, but he left with the lawyers.

The sentences were confirmed on appeal a week later. Unlike the trial, which lasted two to three hours, the appeal lasted twelve hours. This time, the defense lawyers were present and translation was provided.

In October, a second group of blacks was arrested, accused of organizing protests against the arrest of the September group, of raising money for their families and of belonging to FLAM. Nine of the detainees were sentenced to four or five years imprisonment:

Oumar Moussa Bâ, teacher;
Mamadou Bocar Bâ, teacher;
Fara Bâ, teacher;
Ibrahima Khassoum Bâ, customs officer;
Seydou Kane (cousin of the Seydou Kane of the first trial), a student;

[9]Amnesty International, *Mauritania, 1986–1989: Background to a Crisis*, November 30, 1989, p. 15-16.

Kane Abdoul Aziz, an engineer;
Ly Chouaybou, a television producer;
Dia al Hadj, an electrician;
Dia Amadou Tdjane, a student.

A teacher who was part of this second trial told Human Rights Watch/Africa about it. At first, the defendants were not allowed to have a lawyer, the judge questioned the defendants about the alleged activities -- holding demonstrations, burning cars, participating in illegal meetings, distributing tracts inciting blacks to revolt against the government, and being members of FLAM. The teacher also provided details of his detention in an unauthorized detention center, or villa, in Nouakchott:

> While I was in civil prison in Nouakchott, about ten days after my arrival, I was served with what is called an extra action, that is the police came to look for me with an order from the tribunal that authorized them to take me to a special police station -- that is, an unauthorized detention center which in Mauritania is known as villas. The particular villa I was taken to is near the national hospital in an area called zone artesanal, and there I was interrogated by an inspector.
>
> I remained in this villa for a week. I was not subjected to further physical torture but the place was extremely uncomfortable: it was full of mosquitos and extremely cold. Two other people from our group were also served with these extra action orders. All the people who were detained in this unofficial detention center were blacks. No one knew where I was being held during this time because I was not told where I was being taken to when I was taken from the prison. Of course, my family and my friends in the prison were extremely anxious about my whereabouts, and my family got very worried when they came to the prison and brought me food but became aware of the fact that I wasn't in the prison.
>
> Even though I myself was not tortured and neither of the other two members of our group were tortured, I saw other people who were tortured in this villa. One of the methods of torture that was used was to force the detainees to hold up a chair, standing up throughout the night. Most of the blacks who were in this villa had been arrested

because of the political events since September/October 1986. Apart from mosquitos, the cells were filthy and after a week I was transferred back to the civil prison in Nouakchott.[10]

OTHER TRIALS IN 1986 AND 1987

Following the trial of those involved with the 1986 Manifesto, a number of other trials were held in Zouerate, Rosso, Kaedi, and Selibaby in late 1986 and early 1987.

In September 1986, Cpt. Abdoulaye Kébé was tried, allegedly because he provided statistics that were used in the 1986 Manifesto relating to the racial composition of the army. He was held in incommunicado detention, denied access to counsel, and finally tried, *in camera*, before a Special Court of Justice. Reports indicate that he was sentenced to two years in prison and twelve years of internal exile.[11]

In October 1986, another group of blacks was arrested; they were tried in November. In addition to being charged on the same counts as the Manifesto defendants, they were also charged with setting fire to a factory. They were: Ly Moussa, a businessman; Samba Youba, SNIM (the National Mining and Industrial Company); Diallo Alassane, a court assistant; Sarr Gorguo, an engineer; Sy Abdoulaye Malikel, a teacher; and Toumbou Haby, a policeman.

Elsewhere in the country in October 1986, the authorities cracked down on black communities, using mass arrests as a form of intimidation. For example, Mohamed Toure, known as Kaw Tokossel, was arrested in October 1986 at Djowol where his family lives. At the time, he was a secondary school student in Kaedi, eighteen kilometers away, but was home on a school holiday. He explained that after the mass arrests began, a state of emergency was imposed in Djowol because the authorities were looking for those responsible for the troubles, referring to FLAM. He said that students and teachers were a particular target for arrests. The students who were arrested in Djowol attended school in different parts of the country, including Nouakchott and Selibaby. People were picked up everywhere, even the players and crowds at football matches at local stadiums. Those arrested were then taken to Kaedi for interrogation about what they thought of the "events." Arrests and interrogations became a feature of daily life. Individuals were later released but were not

[10]Interview in Dakar, Senegal, February 1991.

[11]Amnesty International, *Mauritania: 1986-1989*, p. 18.

provided with transport to get back to Djowol and other villages.

THE ARREST OF THE MILITARY OFFICERS

On October 17, 1987, the government announced the discovery of a coup plot by a group of black army officers. Fifty-one officers were arrested, held incommunicado and subjected to abusive interrogation tactics, including sleep deprivation. The officers were charged under Articles 83 through 90 of the Penal Code with endangering the security of the state by participating in a conspiracy to overthrow the government and to provoke killing and devastation among the inhabitants of the country.[12] They were denied access to their lawyers until the day of the trial, on November 18. The trial was held according to a special summary procedure that was used when defendants were allegedly caught red-handed.

On December 3, three were sentenced to death; eighteen were sentenced to life imprisonment (including two who died in detention in 1988 due to horrendous prison conditions (see section on "Torture and Prison Conditions," below); nine were sentenced to twenty years; five were sentenced to ten years; three were given five years; six were given five-year suspended sentences with heavy fines; and seven were acquitted. None of those convicted were permitted to appeal.

On December 6, the three army officers sentenced to death were executed. They were: Lt. Sy Saidou, Lt. Bâ Seydi, and Lt. Sarr Amadou.

One of the military officers who was among those arrested gave the following details about the abusive conditions of detention:

> After the execution of my comrades, after spending forty-five days in Jereida, sometimes in individual cells of ninety-by-ninety centimeters, or in collective cells of two-and-a-half-by- three meters, or still others in cells filled with fleas and lice, or finally, in cells for noncommissioned officers and rank and file soldiers. I won't also forget that during the interrogations at Jereida, some of us were locked in places which served as toilets for hours if not days. I will also just mention all that happened in the form of physical torture and murder.[13]

---

[12]Amnesty International, *Mauritania*, p. 21.

[13]Anonymous interview in Nouakchott, Mauritania, September 1991.

An officer who was arrested in October 1987 and released in November told Human Rights Watch/Africa how the policy of dividing the black population helped to secure his release: He was a Soninké, and the government particularly targeted Pulaars.

> I was arrested in Zouerate, and escorted back to Nouakchott under arrest in late October. I was interrogated in Nouakchott, and then taken to Jereida. They wanted to let me go because I was a Soninké. They have a policy to divide the blacks. They tortured my colleagues -- Lt. Niokane was one of them. I was able to escape torture because another officer knew me. I spent three days in prison in Jereida, then held incommunicado in Nouakchott for ten days, before being freed in November.[14]

TORTURE AND PRISON CONDITIONS

Many of the vast numbers of persons arrested because of their presumed association with blacks opposed to the government became victims of torture. Former political prisoners and detainees who described torture commented not only its widespread use, but also on the intensity of its brutality. Release from detention was often accompanied by threats, surveillance and warnings not to leave the country.

In late 1990 and early 1991, the government orchestrated the largest and most brutal round-up of blacks to date: up to 3,000 blacks in the military and civil service were held in incommunicado detention, most of whom were brutally tortured. At least 500 of the detainees died after being summarily executed or tortured to death. (See chapter on "Massacre of 1990-91.") The extent of these atrocities starkly illustrates that there are no limits on the brutality that authorities may inflict on their prisoners with complete impunity.

Most of the cases cited below involve the black political prisoners from the 1986 Manifesto and other trials discussed earlier in this chapter who were held in the prisons in Nouakchott, Nouadhibou, Walata, and Aioun, during the period 1986-1990.

The detainees from the 1986 Manifesto trials were held in the Central Prison in Nouakchott from October 1986 to December 1987. The two groups arrested in September and October 1986 were held separately from each other and were not allowed to have family visits until November 1987. Ibrahima Sall,

---

[14]Interview in Paris, France, November 10, 1991.

who was arrested in September, described the conditions in Nouakchott.

> At first, they put us in with common criminals, but we asked if we [the two groups] could be put together. Two days later, we were transferred into a room with all nineteen of us. It was dirty -- there were no beds, but our families brought us mattresses to sleep on. We were split up into two rooms: the first was about four meters-by-three-and-a-half meters, and forteen of us were there; the second room was about two meters-by-two-and-a-half meters, and five were in there. There were guards at the door and we were only allowed to leave to go to the toilet. The only light we had was from candles, because the windows had been covered.
>
> During our time in Nouakchott, there was no physical mistreatment, just humiliations. It was psychological mistreatment -- you are put in a cell, not allowed to leave, someone with a gun always behind you when you go to the toilet, the psychological tension of overcrowded conditions, going two months without washing, not allowed to see your family, dirty conditions, etc. You are systematically reduced to nothing.
>
> Even common criminals are allowed to see their relatives. We couldn't see anyone -- not even the sun. Fortunately, sometimes we could get books and listen to the radio.
>
> After February 1987, we were transferred to a courtyard, and divided into two groups. Nine of us -- the younger ones -- were put in a cell about three meters by two-and-half meters; next door, the eight others were held. (It was only eight because two were freed after six months). The courtyard was about six meters long, and we could exercise there. Things stayed this way until October 1987, with the coup attempt.

Ibrahima went on to describe how conditions improved, temporarily, when the Baathist prisoners arrived:

> From August 29 until September 15, the Baathists were brought to the prison, and there were eight of them in our cells. They could see their families immediately. We protested, so the lieutenant accepted

> that our families could come. We were allowed to see them for one or two minutes, that's it -- and this only lasted one week, because the Baathists were freed on September 15.
>
> We were able to communicate with the other group of 1986 prisoners through holes in the walls, but we never saw each other. But to let the Baathists communicate with each other, the doors between our cells were opened and we could speak to each other. The day the Baathists left for their trial on the 15th, the doors between the cells were closed.[15]

Incensed by the discrimination apparent in their treatment versus that of the Baathists, the black prisoners wrote an open letter to the President and the other members of the Military Committee of National Salvation. The letter, dated October 3, 1987, detailed the following grievances:

> Our trial revealed a level of discriminatory treatment which has continued into our conditions of detention. These conditions are extremely severe, and are manifested in all sorts of prohibitions. We have been prohibited from communicating with our families, and have been away ever since our sentencing, and some of us had been taken hostage by the police. We were prohibited at a certain point from receiving or buying things necessary for daily life (clothing, soap, candles, sugar, etc.). Our families are completely responsible for our food and medicines. We are denied medical examinations and specialized medical care (arising from a variety of intestinal problems, dental problems, accidents returning from the trial having caused fractures and dislocations, etc.). We are prohibited from moving around in the interior of the prison. We are in permanent reclusion and under surveillance by a guard posted in front of our locked cells, not to mention lack of privacy, the crampedness and unhealthiness of the place. We want you to know that we are taken to the toilets with a machine gun at the back of our necks. We also want you to know about certain security agents who often confuse their political opinions with the laws governing prisons.

---

[15]Interview with Ibrahima Sall in Paris, France, November 1991.

The head of the pro-government Mauritanian League for Human Rights, Ghaly Ould Abdel Hamid, visited the Baathists regularly, but only visited the FLAM prisoners once -- in March 1987, when a representative of the Paris-based International Federation for Human Rights (FIDH) visited them. According to Ibrahima, visits of family and friends were authorized from November 7 until December 9, when the group was transferred to Walata.

Walata, an isolated former French fortress, is infamous for its horrendous prison conditions. Former inmates of Walata, interviewed by Human Rights Watch/Africa, had been subjected to extreme physical and psychological torture, fed inadequate food, forced to live in unsanitary conditions, and received virtually no medical care. In 1988, four political prisoners died in Walata as a result of beri-beri,[16] for which they denied medical attention.

Prisoners described three stages of abuse during their imprisonment at Walata. The first, from December 1987 to March 1988, was psychological, involving the adaptation to the awful conditions and the humiliation of being chained together. The second, from March until April 1988, involved brutal torture sessions. During the third phase, from April until September 1988, the work load was severely increased, sand was put in the food, and the prisoners became ill, leading to the four deaths.

Ibrahima Sall, who spent ten months at Walata, described his experience, including being denied food, chained with other prisoners, forced to perform hard labor, and severely beaten:

> The best way to make people disappear is to send them to Walata, which is almost inaccessible.
>
> We arrived in Walata on the night of December 10-11 -- two days after we left Nouakchott. We were barely fed during the transport -- at one point, we went twelve hours without anything to drink. They took all our things -- our watches, money, everything. Some of our guards were our former students and classmates -- they tortured their own classmates!
>
> After our arrival, we didn't eat until December 12, and then we were given only white rice, no water. Later, we were given water. We were always chained, but eventually we figured out how to open the

---

[16]Beri-beri is a deficiency disease marked by inflammatory or degenerative changes of the nerves, digestive system, and heart.

> locks.
>
> On January 3, they chained our legs. At first, we were chained together in pairs. It was humiliating -- older people were chained to younger ones, and they had to urinate and do everything in front of each other. Soon, the chains began to break our skin.
>
> On January 4, the forced labor began. We built a road. We fetched water -- the well was up hill and our legs were chained together. The chain began to make me bleed, so I asked if they would switch the chain to my other leg. I was chained to Captain Kebe. Lt. Ghaly Ould Souvy came over -- he was arrogant and impolite. He said that we (Captain Kebe and I) were to be brought back to the prison, that I was lazy and didn't want to work....Then he brought us to the torture room. They undressed me, tied my hands behind my back and attached my legs together. They brought a team of four guards; each was to give me sixty lashes on my back. Then the Lieutenant put a pistol to my head and said "we'll kill you here -- we have orders to execute you all."
>
> On the 5th, they stopped chaining us to each other and just chained our legs together.

The twenty-two FLAM prisoners were kept in a cell about two-by-two meters. In April, they were moved to a larger cell, but the windows were covered so it was completely dark. They had to sleep virtually one on top of the other.

Two of the other prisoners, Idrissa and Mamadou, described the overcrowding, lack of sanitation, and misery caused by chaining. The following is their composite testimony:

> We had to sleep on the clay-like ground with a flimsy cover. We were not allowed to take the clothes we had. Each left Nouakchott only with what he was wearing. We were handcuffed the whole time until January 3 and the room was locked all the time. The five Moors and the haratines alone were not handcuffed. There was only one latrine for sixty-six people. During the months that the windows were sealed twenty-four hours a day, the smell was unbearable, especially as people so frequently suffered from dysentery. The

latrine was a room off the big hall.

> We were chained at the legs in groups of two. At first, the haratines (though not the Moors) were chained, but their chains were removed soon afterwards. You were literally stuck with the person you were chained to twenty-four hours a day. They chained older men with much younger which was humiliating for the elderly. They accepted our request that people should at least be chained according to age. After about two weeks, we were chained by ourselves.[17]

Mamadou and Idrissa explained that the prison contained seven areas, the worst being the sixth and seventh where the black political prisoners were held. The Moors, who were common criminals, were kept in the second, which had better toilet facilities, access to water, and less crowded conditions. There were also some black common criminals, who were subjected to severe overcrowding and frequent beatings.

TORTURE

On March 21, 1988, one of the petty criminals was discovered without his chains on and was tortured. After interrogating him, guards learned that other prisoners had learned to remove their chains. That same night they discovered twenty-two of the detainees without chains. All of them were savagely tortured. Ibrahima described the torment of listening to his companions being tortured:

> There's nothing worse than hearing cries and knowing you'll be next. At Walata, they torture for fifteen, thirty, forty-five minutes and you hear terrible screams. Then silence. And you know someone's next. And then they open the door and take one of us.

Idrissa Bâ was one of those severely tortured. He described in detail the torture they were subjected to:

> On the evening of March 21, we were all undressed, chained and hand-cuffed very tightly. We were taken outside in the heat. They opened our mouths, poured sand into our mouths and forced us to swallow by pressing our cheeks. Brig. Chef Mohamed El Habib walked on our heads. It was the responsibility of Cheikh, one of the

[17]Interview in Senegal, May 1990.

> guards who was supposed to work in the infirmary, to point out where we should be hit as we were beaten. Three of the prisoners -- Lt. Diako Abdoul Karim, Lt. Moussa Gomel Barro, Moussa Thioye, a common criminal (Halpulaar) -- were tortured a second time because they were regarded as the key figures behind what the authorities regarded as a "conspiracy" to arrange an escape. They were tortured in front of Lieutenant Dahi, Commander of GRI [*Groupement Regional d'Intervention*].

Ibrahima described the same torture session in March:

> We were taken, our arms tied behind our backs, and stripped. They took us outside at about 8:00 at night. There were about thirty guards in the room -- they hit us with batons and iron cords, then made us lie down and hit us on our backs. I felt like a wild animal with others attacking me, shouting "dirty black" and other insults like "you're all Jews" and "we'll kill you all, exterminate you." It was haratines who beat us. The ones who were beaten the worst were Lt. Diako Abdoul Karim and Lt. Barro Moussa Gomel, of the military prisoners, and Djiby Doua Kamara and Idrissa Bâ of the civilians.
>
> If you resist and you refuse to cry, that humiliates them, and makes them more furious. They are capable of killing you. One man, Sy Mamadou Oumar, got sixty-nine lashes and wouldn't cry.
>
> They would also put a foot on your head, with your nose and mouth in the sand, and kick your head. Once the back of my neck was so swollen from this that there was no indent between the back of my head and my shoulders. And they refused to provide any medical care. They also used "jaguar."[18]

After March 21, all the windows of the big hall were sealed night and day. As a result, many of the prisoners have developed serious eye problems, including Idrissa, who is blind in his left eye. Idrissa explained how conditions deteriorated after March:

---

[18]"Jaguar" is a form of torture in which the detainees are hung over an iron bar, with their hands and feet tied together, and turned on the bar and beaten.

> After March 21, we were *always* chained and hand-cuffed, except for the Moors. Even the pieces of cloth we used for the wounds from the chains were forbidden. From April, it started to get hotter and hotter, but we were not allowed to drink the water that we drew from the well. The only water we were given was a liter for two people, twice a day with food. Nothing else, no matter how thirsty you were. We were denied the water we fetched but watched as the Moor petty criminals washed themselves with this water.

FORCED LABOR

Although only some of the military officers had been sentenced to forced labor, in fact all the FLAM prisoners were subjected to this regime. As Ibrahima explained, the purpose of the forced labor was simply to tire them out. "We'd build a road during the day, then the sand would cover it up and we would have to re-do it. It was like the myth of Sisyphus."

Prisoners were allocated one of two tasks -- either to draw water from a nearby well or to break rocks and transport them. The tasks were alternated. Idrissa Bâ described the hardships of this system.

> Drawing water was particularly harsh because Walata is on top of a steep slope and we had to go up and down a distance of about a kilometer six times every other day, four times in the morning and twice in the later afternoon. We worked in teams of four people. Each team had to bring ninety liters of water. It was extremely difficult to climb up the hill with the chains on. The chains rubbed against the skin and caused wounds. We had to wrap pieces of cloth around our ankles. As we fetched the water, each team was accompanied by a guard who always had his bayonet ready. The guards, all Moors, were always full of insults, "Hurry up, *abiids*."[19]
>
> Even though fewer and fewer people were able to draw water, the quantity of water to be fetched never diminished. Those not too sick to go, though of course everyone was weak, had to go up and down more frequently. The temperature got hotter and hotter, but we were given less water to drink, though we were all weaker each day from lack of food. Three times a day, we were given a teacup (the cups

---

[19]Abiid, meaning slave in Arabic, is a common term of insult against blacks in Mauritania, even though black slavery is practiced mainly in the North.

that are used to drink mint tea in Mauritania are very small).

Another of the FLAM prisoners described the forced labor regime, and the toll that it took on his health.

> At Walata I couldn't walk for about two months, both because of the problem of hunger and the forced labor which we were subjected to. Even when you got food, it was so inedible that you could not eat it. Even just to go to the toilet proved to be too strenuous for me and my friends had to take me to the toilet, basically to carry me there and to carry me back....In my case I think what really finished me off was the labor which we were forced to carry out every day, exacerbated by the extreme lack of food.[20]

DEATHS IN CUSTODY

Preventable deaths were the predictable result of the brutal treatment and the lack of adequate medical care.

In what was described as the third phase of their imprisonment at Walata, the work was intensified and the food was reduced to white rice to which sand was added. The political prisoners grew increasingly weak. Ibrahima noted the differences between the thirty-two civilian FLAM prisoners and the thirty-six military prisoners in their ability to withstand the conditions at Walata. Prior to their transfer to Walata, the civilians had been held in Nouakchott and Nouadhibou, where much of their food was provided by their families. They were also able to bring some money and clothing with them when they were transferred to Walata. The military prisoners, on the other hand, had been arrested in October 1987 and were immediately tortured, poorly fed and hardly had clothes. Accordingly, they were in bad physical shape when they arrived in Walata, and quickly became sick. In 1988, the following prisoners died of beri-beri:

- On August 26, 1988, the first of the prisoners -- Bâ Oumar Alassane -- died. He had become so swollen that his chains had been removed, although no medical care was provided.

- A week later, on September 2, the second prisoner, Tène Youssouf

[20]Interview in Dakar, Senegal, March 1991.

Guèye, died. The day of his death, he was evacuated to Nema for medical treatment, ostensibly to the hospital there, although some reports indicate that he was simply taken to the prison in Nema, where he died.

- On September 13, Bâ Abdoul Khoudouss, a sergeant major, died. Former political prisoners told Human Rights Watch/Africa that the prison authorities refused to allow them to remove his chains before his burial.

- On September 28, Djigo Tafsiro, a former Minister of Heath, died.

One of the prisoners described the indifference of the guards to the deaths:

> On August 26, 1988, at 3:00 P.M., the first of four prisoners died -- Bâ Oumar Alassane, from beri-beri and lack of medical care. He had become terribly swollen, so that the chains had to be taken off. He died in the room with us. When we told Brigadier Ibrahim to take the body away, he replied, "Since you hardly eat any meat, here is your chance." When we said we could not go out that same afternoon to fetch water from the well, he was surprised. "Just because this guy is dead?" We had no choice but to work, and after that, exhausted, we had to bury the corpse some distance away from the prison. Just before he died, we asked the guards for some medicine to reduce his suffering. We knew there was nothing anyway but we were desperate for him. Mustapha, the guard, replied that it was Friday and he could do nothing. The response underlines their utter indifference.
>
> A week later, on September 2, Tène Youssouf Guèye died. He was taken out at about 1:00 A.M. and taken to Nema. He died the same day. He too died of beri-beri. By the time he was evacuated to Nema, he was almost dead. Besides, they did not take him to Nema for medical treatment but simply to deceive us because they took him to the prison in Nema, not the hospital. They just left him in the prison and he was not given *any* medical attention.
>
> In spite of these two deaths in quick succession, conditions did not

change and the situation of all the prisoners got worse and worse.[21]

By the time the fourth prisoner died at Walata, and many of the other prisoners had grown extremely ill, an international campaign had begun focusing on conditions at Walata, sparked by reports from Amnesty International and the press. Shortly thereafter, a few improvements took place. The quality of the food improved somewhat, the Mauritanian Red Crescent[22] sent food and a doctor who stayed for a month, and the windows were unsealed. Although the forced labor regime continued, the prisoners were allowed to drink the water they fetched. In addition to their previous tasks, they were told to start building houses to shelter their families, who were to be allowed to visit them soon. But the houses were never finished because civilians were transferred out of Walata on October 31.

Idrissa, released from Aioun in December 1989, told Human Rights Watch/Africa how close to death many of the prisoners had come:

> If conditions had not changed on October 1, by the 15th everyone would have been dead. We all expected Sarr to be the fifth victim. But even when they gave us more to eat after October 1, we had difficulty in digesting the food. We had been hungry for so long that we ate with great difficulty.

At the time of the international protests about conditions at Walata, the government pretended that it was unaware of the situation and that those guilty of violating the rights of prisoners would be punished. Human Rights Watch/Africa is not aware of any prosecutions of prison officials for deaths resulting from torture or deliberate withholding of medical treatment. However, it is clear that senior government officials were aware of the horrendous conditions at Walata, including the Minister of the Interior at the time, Gabriel Cimper, who himself visited the prison while the abuses were taking place.

After the international pressure surrounding the deaths of the four prisoners, the remaining political prisoners were transferred to another prison, Aioun. Conditions were better in Aioun, as measured by infrastructure, a reduction in torture, better food, no forced labor, and eventual family visits.

---

[21]Interview in Senegal, May 1990.

[22]In Moslem countries, local branches of the Red Cross equivalent are known as Red Crescent.

In Aioun, two or three prisoners shared a cell. The floor was cement and the windows were unsealed. The rooms were not locked during the day, though they were always locked after 9:00 P.M. The latrines were some distance from the rooms, though the prisoners were always accompanied by an armed guard. The meals were terrible at first, but improved somewhat. The prisoners were given rice or wheat and some sauce.

The prisoners were kept from October 31, 1988, to March 4, 1989, without seeing anyone from the outside world in order to allow sufficient time for "rehabilitation."

In late December, the prisoners were allowed radios, but when the ethnic violence exploded in Mauritania and Senegal in April 1989, radios were confiscated. The prisoners were guarded mainly by Moors and a few haratines.

Samba Thiam described the general conditions at Aioun:

> After our transfer to Aioun, we began to receive normal meals -- normal, meaning what regular prisoners got, which sometimes meant a little meat. At Aioun, our treatment depended a lot on which guards were assigned to us. With the change of guards, we had to ask for permission to go to the bathroom and were often insulted. Sometimes we were chained.
>
> Torture was occasional, not systematic. In August 1990, Kane Ibrahima was tortured because he had some problems with the common criminals. He was beaten, and chained for four or five days. Sometimes, with bad guards, we returned to the psychological relations between guards and prisoners like we had at Walata.[23]

In December 1988, three journalists were permitted to visit Aioun. However, conditions were improved specifically for the visit, and the prisoners were not permitted to speak privately to the journalists. Ibrahima Sall described the visit from the journalists.

> On December 3, 1988, we had a visit from some journalists from *Reuters*, *Jeune Afrique*, and *Sud Hebdo*. The day before, on December 2, we were told to undress and were given clothes from the Red Crescent. When the delegation came, we were wearing old

[23]Interview in Dakar, Senegal, February 19, 1991.

> gendarme uniforms. We weren't allowed to speak alone with them, so we designated two of us to speak for us all -- Ibrahima Sarr and Sy Mamadou Youssouf. The governor threatened to torture them, to chain them if the other prisoners [who weren't designated] wouldn't speak. The clinic was stocked with medicine to show the journalists. We wanted to talk to them about our situation, but we weren't permitted. The military prisoners were still at Walata, and the delegation went there as well. The Lieutenant picked two prisoners to speak and threatened to torture them if they discussed conditions [at Aioun or Walata].

Torture did not cease entirely at Aioun. In May 1989, Tayib, an official, used an argument with one of the prisoners, N'gaide Aliou Moctar, an army officer, as an excuse to beat savagely other prisoners who were not involved with the dispute: Thiam Djiby, Chief Warrant Officer; Toumbo Haby; and N'gaide Mamadou Sadio. Aliou Moctar was kept in the punishment cell for more than a week, the others for five days. Ali Moctar suffered a fractured skull.

FAMILY VISITS

Beginning on March 4, family visits were allowed. But given the distance from Nouakchott -- 800 kilometers, about ten hours -- it was very difficult for families to manage such a trip, especially without a place to stay. Nevertheless, they came. Out of a strong sense of solidarity, black families living in the area housed and helped the prisoners' relatives. The visits were limited to thirty minutes in the morning and thirty minutes in the afternoon. But these sessions were entirely at the discretion of the governor and were allotted arbitrarily. Some visitors were allowed to stay longer, others were not allowed at all, or for less than thirty minutes.

A number of wives who managed to visit their husbands in Aioun told Human Rights Watch/Africa that the system was extremely arbitrary and open to corruption; after having traveled such a long distance and endured the ordeal of such a journey, they suddenly found that their "right" to see their husbands depended on their ability to bribe a high prison official.

Despite the difficulties, the visits proved extremely important for the morale of the prisoners. As Ibrahima Sall explained:

> Habsa came on March 8, and I saw her on the 9th. It had been fifteen months and one day since I had seen her. To see people who

love you, who smile at you -- not just guards with guns -- it was especially that which I found most astonishing. Habsa left on March 20, and the events [the expulsions] happened in April.

Habsa Banon, the wife of Ibrahima Sall, described the obstacles faced by families wanting to visit the prisoners:

We often met with the Mauritanian League for Human Rights. He always said that we were allowed to visit our husbands, but he never did anything about it. Finally we were allowed to go, with the permission of the Ministry of the Interior. We took a convoy -- we rented a car for twenty-two of us, and drove the 800 km. for about eight hours. When we arrived, we were told that we could visit for a half an hour per day. So, we went to see the wife of the governor, and explained to her what was happening. The next day, we got permission to stay until 10:00 at night. I stayed one week, from March 8–12.[24]

The wife of another of the prisoners described her visit to Aioun:

The first time I saw him on March 9, 1989, was a shock. He looked so thin and seemed anxious. He had no clothes to speak of. It was clear to all of us that they had delayed family visits from October to March so that they could "fatten" them up and allow their health to improve. But when we saw them, it was terrible. He had no idea about what had happened to any of us; he was not even aware of the death of very close family members, which made the visit an even sadder occasion.

During that first visit, which is the only one I made before I was deported, we stayed ten days. We were not allowed to remain more than an hour during any one visit and even then, the visit could suddenly be terminated. We stayed in the homes of black gendarmes working in the area. We learned subsequently that they had problems on account of that. Many of the prisoners no longer have close family members living in Mauritania because so many people have been deported. Because even those who remain in Mauritania do not

---

[24]Interview with Habsa Banon in Paris, France, November 8, 1991.

have news of the prisoners; no one dares to visit them as there is no security.[25]

[25]Interview in Senegal, May 1990.

9
Democratization

The democratization process in Mauritania began in April 1991, when President Taya announced plans for a new constitution and multiparty elections. The government's decision was sparked by its concerns over criticism by the international community in the wake of the 1990-91 massacre, and the need to demonstrate reforms in order to qualify for much-needed foreign aid. However, although a few cosmetic steps were taken toward democratization and government-instigated violence abated in 1992, Mauritania has retained all the apparatus of a repressive state with a disregard for basic human rights.

A Mauritanian teacher noted the difference between the changes on paper and the reality for the people, as follows:

> The situation remains the same. Maybe those who are abroad and who read the papers and declarations and ordinances and presidential decrees can think that the situation is improving. But that is not the case. What is said on the radio is different from what is really happening.[1]

The U.S. State Department's *Country Report's on Human Rights Practices for 1992* echoed this sentiment, noting that the elections were "flawed" and that the political situation was still tightly controlled. It said:

> This quasi-transformation of the Taya Government from a military regime to one with a more civilian cast failed to satisfy the political opposition's demands for a truly democratic system. Although the new Constitution and attendant ordinances permitted political parties and an independent press to operate, for example, both of these freedoms were limited. Taya's party totally dominated Parliament, the newspapers were subject to a strict libel law, and the Government continued to monopolize radio and television.

The first test of the government's commitment to democratization came in April and May 1991, when a series of open letters were issued calling on the government to allow an independent investigation of the massacre of 1990-91 and to institute democratic reforms (see chapter on "The Massacre of 1990-

---

[1]Anonymous interview in Nouakchott, Mauritania, September 1991.

1991"). The government did not engage in immediate reprisals against the signatories of these letters.

In June, several Moors who had signed one of the letters were arrested. Their arrests were related to involvement in a new political organization, the United Democratic Front of Forces for Change (Front démocratique uni des forces de changement -- FDUC), which was formed in June by a group of opposition movements and individuals. The president of the Front was Hadrami Ould Khattry; the vice presidents were Messaoud Ould Boulkheir and Diop Mamadou Amadou. Those arrested were: Diop Mamadou Amadou, former minister of education; Messaoud Ould Boulkheir, former minister of rural development and candidate for mayor of Nouakchott in 1990; Moustapha Ould Bederdine; Béchir el Hassan, journalist; Ladji Traoré, economist and former political prisoner; Hadrami Ould Khattry, former minister of education; and Abderrahmane el Yassa. They were initially taken to the Ministry of the Interior, after which they were put in a truck and driven to Kiffa, where they were split into three groups and taken to separate locations: Ould Boulkheir and Diop Mamadou went to Tichit; Abderahmane Ould Yessa and Béchir El Hassen to Tamcheket; Ould Bedredine and Traore to Boundeit; and Ould Khattry to Oudane.[2] They were all held in incommunicado detention until July 25.

THE JULY 1991 REFERENDUM ON THE DRAFT CONSTITUTION

As President Taya had promised in his April speech, a referendum was held on July 12, 1991, to decide whether a draft constitution would replace the constitution suspended after the 1978 coup. The draft constitution proclaimed Mauritania's attachment to Islam as well as to the principles of democracy as set forth in the Universal Declaration of Human Rights and the African Charter on Human and Peoples Rights. It provided for the president, who must be Muslim, to be elected by universal suffrage, for an unlimited number of political parties. It further stated that the official language is Arabic, and that the national languages are Pulaar, Soninké, and Wolof.

Official results stated that the referendum passed by 97.94 percent, with 85 percent of the eligible voters participating. These figures were disputed by opposition groups, which had called a boycott that was widely observed. The opposition contended that the voter turnout was greatly exaggerated by the government. Many blacks also complained that the voting cards and lists of voters were written only in Arabic. Reports from Nouakchott indicated that

---

[2]Interview in New York, April 21, 1992.

most of those who voted were Moors, and that voter turnout was considerably lower than the government indicated.

The opposition had called the boycott because they claimed that the draft constitution discriminated against blacks, gave too much power to the president, and did not set presidential term limits. Of particular concern was Article 18, which stipulated a number of security-related duties and crimes that were open to misinterpretation by the authorities. The article states:

> All citizens have the duty to protect and safeguard the independence, sovereignty, and territorial integrity of the country. Treason, espionage, passing to the enemy as well as all infractions committed against the security of the state will be punished to the full extent of the law.

The opposition objected to the military government's lack of consultation with the opposition in the drafting of the Constitution, and argued that a transitional government should have been appointed to administer the elections. The opposition also charged that the referendum was taking place in an atmosphere of intimidation, given that several of the opposition leaders remained in incommunicado detention. A spokesperson for FLAM, Seri Bâ, summed up the opposition's position for Radio France International:

> As far as we are concerned, the referendum is simply an accident of history. It is simply null and void as long as those who have been gagged and tied up are not rehabilitated and back in the country. We also recall our demands: first, the holding of a national conference, then the setting up of an international investigating commission which will shed light on the crimes committed since 1986. And we think that decisions that would restore peace and trust in Mauritania should be taken...[3]

The call for a boycott was echoed in an appeal by 4,267 women refugees in Senegal. In a statement released in Dakar, the group stated that "any democratization process is only possible in Mauritania...once national reconciliation is restored."

NEW LEGISLATION

Following the referendum, the government instituted a number of

---

[3]Radio France International, July 12, 1992, reprinted in BBC, *Summary of World Broadcasts*, July 15, 1991.

liberalizing measures, including an amnesty for political prisoners. In late July, new laws were promulgated on political parties and the press. The law on political parties states that any Mauritanian of voting age may join a political party, but that all parties must abstain from propaganda "in contradiction with the principles of true Islam," and that no party "can carry the banner of Islam alone." The law further states that parties are prohibited from being formed on a racial, regional, or tribal basis.[4] Chapters four and five of the law enable the government to suspend or dissolve political parties if they do not comply with the regulations.

The press law states that the press must adhere to principles "based on tolerance, respect for others, fairness, just treatment and upholding the principles of freedom, social justice and the defense of human rights and for justice among nations..."[5] It goes on to note that the offense of insulting the President of the Republic is punishable by imprisonment and fines.

Despite the new press law, the September 1991 issue of the journal *Mauritanie Demain*, an independent paper, was banned for an article reporting that black detainees had been tortured to death. Mubarak Ould Beirouk, the magazine's editor, said he was told that the article was divisive and "endangered national unity."[6]

In July 1992, individuals closely associated with the government sued two of the most outspoken journals, *Al Bayane* and *L'Eveil Hebdo*. The case against *Al Bayane* was brought by the administrator of a private school in Nouakchott because of an article about corruption in the school. The case against *L'Eveil Hebdo* was brought by a relative of the President, Hadramy Ould Taya, concerning an article on the post-election violence in Nouadhibou which reported that one of the demonstrators was killed by a bullet that may have come from his home. Both plaintiffs won their cases, but the damages awarded were not substantial.

Still, the most positive aspect of Mauritania's democratization is that the independent press became a more vibrant force since 1992. Independent journalists are given wider latitude today than ever before to investigate and write about government abuses, both past and present.

---

[4]BBC, *Summary of World Broadcast*, July 27, 1991.

[5]BBC, *Summary of World Broadcasts*, July 29, 1991.

[6]Sheikh Bekaye, "Magazine Banned for Reporting Charges of Torture, Executions," *The Associated Press*, September 2, 1991.

THE PRESIDENTIAL ELECTIONS

During the months preceding the elections that were scheduled for January 1992, most opposition parties were allowed to register.[7] By December 1991, at least eleven political parties had registered, but virtually all had close links to the ruling authorities. One, the Social Democratic Republican Party (SDRP), was formed at the end of August 1991 by President Taya. Another, the Assembly for Democracy and National Unity, was formed the same month by Ahmed Ould Sidi Baba, the mayor of Atar and a relative of Taya.[8] The only genuine opposition parties were the Union of Democratic Forces, which includes beydanes, haratines and representatives of black ethnic groups, and the Party for Freedom, Equality, and Justice, which was formed in late November 1991 and is largely black.

The opposition ultimately coalesced around Ahmed Ould Daddah, the candidate of the Union of Democratic Forces (UFD).[9] Ould Daddah, an economist and half brother of Mauritania's first president, Moktar Ould Daddah, ran on a platform of a "new era" and national reconciliation; he attracted the support of most of the black voters, who saw him as the only alternative to Taya.

Although the opposition was not prevented from campaigning, President Taya was able to use many of the state's resources to further his campaign, including the state bureaucracy and the national airline, Air Mauritanie. Taya's

---

[7]Among the parties officially registered are: the Popular Social Democratic Union, the Mauritanian Renewal Party, the Union of Democratic Forces, the Democratic Justice Party, the Mauritanian Center Democratic Party, the Socialist Popular Democratic Union, the National Vanguard Party.

However, an Islamic party, the Islamic Ummah Party, was refused permission to register, based on the constitutional provision which bans the formation of religious parties.

[8]Some of the other political parties are: The New Mauritanian Party, headed by Moulaye Zeyd, a former mayor of Zourate; the People's Social and Democratic Union, headed by Mohammed Mahmoud Ould Mah, a former mayor of Nouakchott; and the Party for Democratic Justice, headed by Mohammed Abdoullahi Ould El Bane, a beydane professor.

[9]Other candidates were Moustapha Ould Saleck, the colonel who overthrew President Moktar Ould Daddah in 1978, and Mohamed Mahmoud Ould Mah, an economist and former mayor of Nouakchott.

campaign promised "change with stability."

ELECTORAL MALPRATICE

Electoral malpractice began with voter registration. Many blacks and supporters of the opposition were prevented from registering, using a variety of tactics. The UFD estimates that some 25,000 people were not able to register in Nouakchott alone. In some districts, the prefect simply refused to register blacks, who had no recourse available to enforce their rights. Intimidation tactics were also used. Special forces of the army were deployed around registration sites and sometimes engaged in violence, reportedly including tear gas and beatings to disperse those who had gathered to register. When asked how the authorities knew who supported the opposition and who backed the government, a UFD spokesman expressed his view of how the government kept voter registration under its control:

> If you see a black, you know he's in the opposition. If you see a haratine, there's a 75 percent chance. For Arabs it's more difficult, but Moors from opposition areas were also prevented from registering, especially in Boutlimit [where Ould Daddah is from].[10]

One method used to prevent blacks from registering was to demand to see their identity cards, which many of them did not have. The authorities had effectively stopped issuing I.D.s to blacks in the late 1980s.

Another method was to ask questions in Arabic, which many blacks were not able to speak or understand. One man interviewed by Human Rights Watch/Africa gave the following account of the difficulty he and his aunt had in trying to register.

> We got on line. There were two lines -- one for men, one for women. We went to another department of Nouakchott to register, because we had heard that the prefect in our district wasn't allowing blacks to register. They can do that by asking you questions that are impossible to answer.
>
> My aunt doesn't speak Arabic (she doesn't speak French either; she's illiterate), so I wrote the number of our house on a piece of paper for her. She was asked to name the head of the district (*chef du quartier*). She

[10] Interview in New York, April 23, 1992.

> didn't understand, but she presented the piece of paper. Since she couldn't answer the question, she was taken outside by guards. I took her home.[11]

The man went on to describe how they then went to another district where they had heard there was a more sympathetic prefect, and eventually they were registered.

Even managing to register did not guarantee that one would be permitted to vote. When the voting cards were being distributed, many blacks were denied their cards on various pretexts, such as their names being spelled differently on the electoral lists and I.D. cards; mismatched numbers on the cards and lists; and the same registration number being used by more than one person. In some instances, the authorities simply did not bring the list of registered voters, or claimed to have lost the registration cards. "There was total disorder, with thousands of people waiting," one man explained. "But we felt that the only way to have our freedom was to vote. So we waited all day for our cards." His account of obtaining his voting card illustrates the frustrations involved in the process:

> I got my card on the third day. I waited for two days from 5:00 A.M. until midnight, and finally, at about 10:30 P.M. on the third day, I got in. They found my card, but there was a missing number. They told me to come back, but I said there was no way I was coming back -- they had to give me my card now. They looked in their lists and checked around -- it took more than one-and-a-half-hours to find my number! But they finally found it, and wrote it on my voting card. This was Tuesday night; the elections were Friday.

The French daily *Le Monde* gave the following summary of the conduct of the elections:

> One thing is clear and, to be frank, hardly surprising: there were numerous and flagrant irregularities. These were not all due to the lack of means and know-how of the administration. Among other anomalies, the UFD also revealed that in ten towns, the number of those registered surpassed the number of people of voting age and, in two districts, the number

---

[11]Interview in New York, March 12, 1992.

actually exceeded the total population.[12]

POST-ELECTION VIOLENCE

After the January 24, 1992, elections, a curfew was announced and a crackdown on opposition activists was launched, leading to the arrest of opposition supporters in various parts of the country, including Nouadhibou, Nouakchott, Rosso, and Kaedi. In addition, government forces violently attacked opposition activists in Nouadhibou and Nouakchott, including members of the UFD who were demonstrating in Nouadhibou on January 26. As a result, Ousmane Traore, Samba Diallo, and possibly as many as three other UFD supporters were killed. Scores of UFD supporters in Nouadhibou were rounded up, and twenty-seven of them were imprisoned on charges of inciting violence. They were released in early February and all charges were dropped. On January 25, the security forces used tear gas to attack the UFD headquarters in Nouakchott, injuring twenty.

LEGISLATIVE ELECTIONS

In March 1992, legislative elections were held. Again, the opposition boycotted, citing the conduct of the presidential elections and the government's refusal to meet the opposition's conditions, such as postponing the elections to permit the political parties to adequately prepare; revising the electoral lists; creating a commission to supervise the elections; and forming an independent commission of inquiry to investigate the post-election killings in Nouadhibou. The president and his party thus retained control of the country.

According to the report of Klaus Kübler, a German parliamentarian, approximately two-thirds of the 1.2 million eligible voters did not vote. Kübler had been invited to observe the legislative elections, just as he had observed the presidential elections, but he and the other observers refused to participate in light of the opposition boycott. In a statement released after the elections, he wrote: "This verdict of non-voters against the party of the former head of state, the only party to participate in the elections, made the electoral result a real democratic farce." He went no to sum up the state of democracy in Mauritania:

> After the presidential and legislative elections in Mauritania, President Taya succeeded, using questionable means, in concentrating enormous

[12] Jacques de Barrin, "Mauritanie: la démocratie à l'épreuve des tensions raciales," *Le Monde*, (Paris), March 6, 1992.

power in his hands. In effect, the president or his party have a monopoly on virtually all the important political positions -- in parliament, the second chamber, the Senate and the Constitutional Council. In addition, the constitution gives the president strong powers. Under these conditions, it is difficult to talk of democratization in Mauritania.

On January 28, 1994, the first round of municipal elections were held, in which the opposition participated. A second round was held on February 4. According to the official results, the PRDS, the president's party, carried the majority of the country, winning in 172 of the 208 municipalities; the UFD won 17; other parties won 19.[13] The president of the UFD, Ould Daddah, denounced what he called "massive fraud" during the elections. A protest march that the UFD tried to organize on February 10 was prohibited by the authorities.[14]

[13]"Elections municipales: le PRDS, le parti au pourvoir, renforce ses positions," *Agence France-Presse*, February 2, 1994.

[14]"Interdiction d'une marche de l'opposition," *Agence France-Presse*, February 11, 1994.

10
THE SENEGAL RIVER VALLEY UNDER MILITARY OCCUPATION

Ever since the conflict with Senegal in 1989, an undeclared state of emergency has been in place along the Senegal River Valley, including a military occupation and an unofficial night curfew. A chronic and insidious pattern of violations against black Mauritanians, including indiscriminate killing, detention, torture, rape, and beating by the military and militia forces stationed in the valley has been the result. The abuses have been associated with attempts to seize land owned by blacks, expel them from the country, deny their civil rights, and institutionalize control over them.

Though mass expulsions had ended early in 1989, the military continued to expel smaller numbers of black Mauritanians throughout the year, and increased the rate of expulsions in the first half of 1990. In addition, as a result of the continuing abuses, black villagers and herders have continued to flee Mauritania in search of refuge in Senegal or Mali. Their farmland is confiscated for future ownership by Moors.

The Senegal River Valley has been transformed. Houses formerly inhabited by blacks have been emptied and are now occupied by Moors; fields that had been tended for generations by black villagers are now owned by white Moor businessmen and are frequently worked by haratines; and even the names of some of these villages have been changed,[1] erasing the last traces of the former proprietors.

While the rate of killings has clearly diminished since 1992, the remaining black populations continue to face great difficulty obtaining official identity documents, jobs, bank loans, and land. The unofficial curfew prevents a return to normal ways of life, especially for the farmers and herders. No semblance of the rule of law exists for blacks. Freedom of movement within the country is also restricted. Blacks describe near-certain harassment at the numerous checkpoints along the major roads. Whether they are in private cars or in public transportation, blacks are singled out by the military and police, often forced to show their identification papers and subjected to searches of their luggage, and sometimes detained.

---

[1]One example cited by refugees is a village on the Senegal River that used to be called Vindé Thiloude; its name has been changed to Dar el Beyda, which means "the white house." Another example is the village known as Nima, which is now called Dar es Salaam.

The elections of 1992 did little to improve the situation, especially for blacks in the Senegal River Valley. "The fear is visceral," explained Samba, a Mauritanian exile in Dakar. "Despite the democratization, there is no sense of security. The blacks live in fear that at any moment they could be repressed. It's always there."[2] According to another black Mauritanian: "This is not democracy. It is demagoguery."[3]

CONTINUED CONFLICT OVER LAND

One of the main reasons for the army's occupation of the valley has been to continue the process of confiscating land from the black population there. The presence of soldiers and the enforcement of a *de facto* state of emergency have greatly assisted beydanes who wish to acquire land. Not only have the continuing abuses against the farmers of the valley caused many of them to flee and abandon their land, but the ready availability of soldiers has facilitated the forcible seizures of land from the black farmers who remain.

An example of the determination of the government to continue seizing land, and the desperation of the remaining black farmers to hold onto it, occurred in September 1991, in a village called Sylla, near Kaedi. The previous month, the governor had taken land that belonged to a black cooperative and given it to an unidentified businesswoman from Nouakchott. On September 9, the head of the cooperative met with the prefect of Kaedi and other officials to explain that the ninety hectares given by the governor encroached upon the fifty hectares that the cooperative had registered. The prefect made it clear that the governor's decision was final. On September 10, blacks from the cooperative organized a sit-in to protest the transfer of land and to block initial efforts to develop the land. The village chief explained to a journalist from the French daily, *Le Monde*, what had driven them to stage the protest:

> The authorities have already taken our lands to distribute to those expelled from Senegal. There was no way we could sit by and watch more lands be taken away. This is our land on which we planned to build a cooperative.[4]

---

[2]Interview in Dakar, Senegal, October 24, 1993.

[3]Interview in Department of Podor, Senegal, October 31, 1993.

[4]Jacques de Barrin, "Kaedi entre ses mauvais souvenirs et ses bonnes terres," *Le Monde*, (Paris), March 22-23, 1992.

The following day, the captain of the National Guard picked up the village chief, Athie Seydou Thierno, and five other villagers and said he was taking them to meet with the governor. Reports indicate that the six men were taken directly to Kaedi's central police station, and negotiations never took place. Meanwhile, the governor ordered security forces to be deployed; they later opened fire on the protestors, leaving three blacks dead and five wounded.[5] The incident was reported in the local press, including the pro-government journal *Le Temps*.

The experience of N'Diorol, a village in the Boghé department, illustrates the lengths to which some black villagers have gone in attempting to save their land.[6] The inhabitants of N'Diorol are farmers, and in 1978, the village cooperative began cultivating a field of sixteen hectares. In 1988, they requested an extension of twenty hectares, which was granted, and they began farming it in 1989.

That same year, the regional director of the National Corporation for Rural Development (SONADER), Cheikh Moussa, informed the villagers that he had received instructions to take back the first field, and the motorpump that was situated on it. These were given to haratines, whom the government claimed were repatriated, that is, expelled from Senegal, but whom the villagers assert were members of the cooperative who had always lived there. On March 10, 1989, the villagers wrote to the Minister of the Interior, Post, and Telecommunications in Nouakchott, describing how certain Moors were attempting to expropriate their land. Their letter included the following description of the injustices they were experiencing:

> We notified the local authorities to put an end to this expropriation, which has neither a legal justification nor follows any sort of legal procedure, and which constitutes an extreme injustice. Up to the present, we have received no response, and the situation is going from bad to worse....We ask you to intervene quickly to stop this arbitrary action and to prevent any problems from exploding.

---

[5]M. Abdelllahi and M. R. C. Bounena, "Tuerie de Sylla," *Le Temps*, #11, (Nouakchott), September 22-28, 1991.

[6]This information is based on the letters written by the villagers of N'Diorol to the local and national authorities between 1989 and 1993, as well as interviews conducted in the Department of Podor in October 1993.

In February 1990, the cooperative sought a further extension of twenty hectares. The haratines then asked for the same plot, and the authorities granted the haratines' request. The government said again that the haratines were among those expelled from Senegal; the villagers again contended that they had always lived there. More letters and visits to local officials followed. In May 1993, the villagers requested another hectare extension. As of November 1993, they had received no response to this request. On September 13, 1993, the villagers wrote again to the Minster explaining their efforts since March 1989 to block the expropriation of their land, but to no avail.

EXTRAJUDICIAL EXECUTIONS

Blacks, particularly those who live along the Senegal River Valley, are afraid to leave their homes after dusk. In some areas, the local military commanders reportedly told the villagers that they would shoot whoever was found outside at night. One black Mauritanian reported that the villagers in the Bogué department were told in October 1993 by the commander of the military base that anyone found near the river after 6:00 P.M. would be shot.

The following cases of extra-judicial killings were reported to Human Rights Watch/Africa:

- In August 1993, Abass Demba from Helbir Village went to Kaedi to sell some cattle and was accused of being Senegalese. He was arrested and taken to the gendarmerie, where he was beaten so badly that he had to be hospitalized. Some villagers tried unsuccessfully to see him. His body was later found by a fisherman in the Senegal River near Gababe.[7]

- In July or August 1993, Samba Kibo, a herder, was killed by gendarmes between Kabou and Selibaby. He had gone to the gendarme headquarters after his herds had been stolen. The gendarmes took him in their vehicle to look for the herds and then shot him. The family found the body and learned what happened after bribing a gendarme. One gendarme was arrested in connection with the killing, but he was released two weeks later.[8]

---

[7]Interview in the Department of Matam, Senegal, October 30, 1993.

[8]Interview the Department of Matam, Senegal, October 30, 1993.

- On the night of March 14, 1993, a forty-three-year-old man named Thiampane was shot by the military while fishing in the Senegal River.[9]

- In January 1993, Simbing Sow and Demba Sow, both herders, were killed between Selibaby and Sanghediere. They were suspected of trying to cross to Senegal with their animals. Their herds were stolen.[10]

- In June 1992, Moussa Boudou Dia, a sixty-three-year-old shepherd, was killed near Touroula and his herd was stolen. His family complained to the authorities and even went to see the governor of Selibaby, but there was no response.[11]

- On the night of February 21-22, 1992, Oumar Diop was killed near Boghé. He drowned after being thrown in the water by security forces who intercepted him and his brother, Ibrahima Diop, as they were entering the village. Oumar Diop's family called on the authorities to investigate the murder.[12]

- In 1991, Ifra Mamedou Deh and Abdoulaye Demba Deh, both Peul herders, were killed by the military in the bush near the village of Sounnatou. Their herds were taken by the military.[13]

According to our information, no official investigations have been conducted into these killings, which indicates that the security forces are permitted to kill with impunity.

---

[9]Interview in the Department of Podor, Senegal, October 31, 1993.

[10]Interview in the Department of Matam, Senegal, October 30, 1993.

[11]Interview in the Department of Bakel, Senegal, October 28, 1993.

[12]"Mise au point de la famille Diop à 'Horizons,'" Nouakchott: *Eveil Hebdo*, March 23, 1992.

[13]Interview in the Department of Bakel, Senegal, October 28, 1993.

MILITARY REPRISALS AGAINST CIVILIANS

Militias comprised of haratines have joined the security forces as part of the apparatus of repression. Since bands of deported Peul herders began to launch raids from Senegal and Mali to reclaim their herds, and sometimes simply to steal animals from the Moors, the militias have been used to pursue the raiders, referred to as "bandits," to the border. If the bandits succeed in crossing the border, the security forces frequently take reprisals against black civilians in local villages. Reprisals sometimes take the form of public humiliations of village elders or women; at other times the vengeance leads to killings.

Authorities cite the Peul raiders as a reason for arbitrarily attacking blacks, whom they accuse of being or collaborating with bandits. This blanket charge is used all along the valley, but especially in the area of Guidimaka where raids from refugees in Mali and Senegal are more frequent.

The examples cited to Human Rights Watch/Africa of black villagers being accused of banditry include the following:

- In September or October 1993, Yali Kone, a Peul herder, was arrested and taken to the military base in Gasra, where he was beaten so badly that his hearing was damaged. He was accused of helping bandits steal cattle.[14]

- Abdoulaye was arrested by the gendarmes in Kiffa in late 1989, accused of banditry. He was not permitted to see a lawyer or to contact his family, and was never brought to trial. He was finally released in the spring of 1993, and he fled to Senegal.[15]

There are also many reports of the National Guard and the gendarmes imposing "taxes" on villages for alleged collaboration with the "bandits." Similarly, Moors who lose their cattle to "bandits" are reportedly often permitted to take the cattle of black villagers. For example, in the village of Aéré Mbar in the Department of Bababé in August 1993, the cows of a Moor were taken; he then took cattle from the village and kept them until his cows

[14]Interview in the Department of Podor, Senegal, October 31, 1993.

[15]Interview in the Department of Bakel, Senegal, October 28, 1993.

were returned.[16]

Soldiers often take the villagers' food, their livestock, their belongings. One refugee from Selibaby commented:

> Most people fleeing now do it on their own -- they are not being forced to cross [the river]. They are leaving to be with their families, or because life there is just too hard. They find themselves with nothing: their animals are wrenched away from them, all their belongings are taken, as well as their food. The military lives off them and demands food. You cannot defend yourself against the state. You cannot refuse to give the soldiers what they want.[17]

An example of villages being "invaded" in this manner is that of Tagou Talla and Diarebé.[18] In late February 1991, the military reportedly arrived and demanded that the villagers' goods and personal belongings be handed over. As is often the case, many of the young men of the village were arrested. In this case, some eleven herders and farmers were arrested, including: Bâ Oumar Oumouyel, the seventy-year-old village chief; the chief's brother, Bâ Sirou, and the chief's thirty-three-year-old son, Bâ Mamadou Oumar. Others arrested were: Bâ Mamadou Demba, thirty-two years old; Gadio Amadou Hamadi, thirty-three years old; Bâ Amadou Mody, thirty years old; Bâ Doro Samba, forty years old; Amadou Demba Bary, forty-four years old; Bâ Samba Abou, twenty-eight years old; Hawa Hamadi, a twenty-year-old woman; and Bâ Ifra Boye, twenty-five years old.

ARBITRARY ARREST AND DETENTION

Frequently, if blacks are caught by security forces and cannot produce identity cards to prove that they are Mauritanian, they are either detained or beaten and forced to cross the river to Senegal. "Things are better now," one refugee pointed out when discussing these arbitrary arrests. "In 1989, these people would have been killed. Now, they [the military] beat you badly and

---

[16] Interview in Dakar, Senegal, November 3, 1993.

[17] Interview in the Department of Bakel, Senegal, February 27, 1991.

[18] Interview in the Department of Bakel, Senegal, February 27, 1991.

then let you go. We think things are good now."[19]

The following cases illustrate the ongoing pattern of arbitrary arrests and beatings:

- In June 1993, Ba Ousmane Samba, a refugee in Senegal, crossed back into Mauritania to get his wife and bring her back to Senegal. He was arrested by gendarmes when he could not produce his identity papers and taken to the police station in Djoel. The gendarmes took all his money -- some 20,000 CFA -- and forced him to cross back to Senegal.[20]

- In May-June 1993, Demba Dondou, a refugee in Senegal in his late twenties, went to Kaedi to see his uncle. He was arrested by gendarmes and beaten.[21]

- One young refugee from N'Djavelil crossed to Mauritania in May 1993 to get his animals. He was caught by the military and beaten, before being sent back to Senegal. "I went back this year because I thought all was calm. It was my first visit back -- and my last," he said.[22]

Salif, a man in his mid-twenties from the village of Mbomé, described how he was arrested and tortured and eventually forced to leave the country, as follows:

> I was arrested in May 1990 with several others from my village -- Amadou Tougoudé, Diobo Bâ, Lairie Bâ, Amadou Lairie Bâ (the son of Lairie Bâ), Hodou Demba Diallo, Saidou Koumba. We were tied up and taken away in cars. They beat us repeatedly on our feet with their guns. We finally arrived at the military camp in Luggere Pooli Bodeeji. We had to sleep on the ground. We were still tied up, and

[19]Interview in the Department of Podor, Senegal, October 31, 1993.

[20]Interview in the Department of Matam, Senegal, October 30, 1993.

[21]Interview in the Department of Matam, Senegal, October 30, 1993.

[22]Interview in the Department of Bakel, Senegal, October 27, 1993.

sometimes the soldiers walked on us. We were beaten during the night, and not allowed to eat or drink.

We were finally untied by armed guards. They began to pull the hair out of our beards, our heads, all over. We were also beaten while suspended. Two other people from the village of Gurel Jahjahbe were also there and were being tortured, but for less time than us, one day. We were held for four days. We were arrested because we were Halpulaars; they accused us of being linked to the commandos from Senegal [expellees who return to Mauritania to recapture confiscated property and sometimes attack Mauritanian soldiers].

Our families went to the authorities in Selibaby, all the way up to the governor. Our village elders brought gifts to the authorities. We were uniquely fortunate -- the military released us. Others died because of the torture.

When the military was ordered to release us, we were taken to Selibaby, where the prefect took us to a hospital and we were cared for discreetly. We were then sent to the police station, where we were imprisoned for four days. We were told to leave the country and never to tell anyone what happened.[23]

ABUSES AGAINST WOMEN

Black women in Mauritania are subject to sexual harassment and other forms of abuse. One woman who crossed to Senegal in January 1993 told Human Rights Watch/Africa that women fear harassment by the military when traveling between the markets and their homes.[24] Other refugees said that women milk sellers face arrest if they cannot produce their identification papers.

There are consistent reports of rapes all along the valley, although they are difficult to document because of the shame associated with rapes. In late July 1993, for example, five women in the village of Koundel in the region of Gorgol were reportedly abducted for two days by the military, during which

[23]Interview in the Department of Bakel, Senegal, February 27, 1991.

[24]Interview in the Department of Bakel, Senegal, October 28, 1993.

time they were raped.[25] Villages along the river report that soldiers from the military bases go to black villages at night and take young women back to the bases. Some refugees cite a large number of births of "white" babies along the valley as proof of systematic rapes by the military.

INDIRECT EXPULSIONS

Some blacks continue to flee Mauritania because of ongoing abuses. In the region of Bakel alone, a refugee organization estimates that 547 black Mauritanians crossed over to Senegal between April and October 1993,[26] a clear indication that problems remain.

Amadou, the chief of a village in the Guidimakha region, fled Mauritania in May 1993 along with fifty others. He described continuous problems with the military, ranging from demands for payment of arbitrary "taxes" in the form of money, cows, or goats, to arbitrary arrests and killings of Peul herders. "This is the life of blacks in Mauritania," he said. "They all wish to leave -- not because they want to, but because of the conditions."[27] He went on to describe how the abuses had reduced the village by more than three-quarters:

> I wanted to leave since 1989, but since I am responsible for 133 families in the village, I had to stay. Of the 133 families, there were no deportations, but they [the military] took our herds, and people began to leave on their own, beginning in 1989 and continuing until now. About thirty families are still there.
>
> Since 1989, the military has come to the village and demanded payment in the form of money or animals. Even if you complain, it's no use. I kept a list of all that was taken by the military, and I wrote to the mayor of Selibaby in 1991. The response: the gendarmes were sent to see me, and then they started taking things, and were even worse than the military. They even imposed taxes for the wood we used. Sometimes people would be arrested, and we would have to pay bribes to get them back.

---

[25]Interview in the Department of Matam, Senegal, October 30, 1993.

[26]Interview in the Department of Bakel, Senegal, October 27, 1993.

[27]Interview in the Department of Bakel, Senegal, October 28, 1993.

A blind religious leader interviewed by Human Rights Watch/Africa explained that he left Mauritania on May 7, 1990, "because we were tired and afraid." He continued: "When you know our problems in depth, you understand that we had no choice but to leave."

> Above all else, these villagers are peasants. They just want to live in peace; they have no political ambitions. Without understanding why, they saw the authorities -- angry, coming to see them, taking their sheep and belongings. The authorities would say "give me your sheep" -- they don't ask, they order.
>
> The Moors harassed people in the village -- interrogating them, sometimes taking them for long periods and torturing them. Some would come back in bad shape. One man, Birama Dia, was killed. It seemed as though this period lasting a long time. Finally, the whole village decided to leave.

He went on to relate that the villagers were driven out of the temporary villages they had erected near the fields where they were harvesting. After they returned to their villages, they were so harassed by the Moors that they decided to flee to Senegal. He described what happened to a group of about sixty of them who got separated from the rest.

> The military found us, and took us to the military camp. We were shot at and one of my students was hit in the hand, and then fled out of fear. Since I am blind, I was left with two children about 12-years-old. We were tied up and tortured -- hit with guns, kicked all over our bodies. All our goods were taken. We were in the camp for about two days.
>
> Finally, some authorities from the regional capital, Selibaby, came and we were released. They told us to cross [the river]. Several of those who tried to cross died, either of thirst on their way to the river or were shot: Oumar Tall, ten years old; Dado Ndow, Hamady Beydary, almost seventy years old; Aissata Deenaba, about forty years old with her two-year-old baby; Rougui Ndongo, about fifteen

years old; Abdul Moussa Njang, about eight years old.[28]

THE REFUGEES

The expellees -- now refugees -- have been in Senegal for nearly five years. When they first arrived, they pinned their hopes for return on the Senegalese government, never believing that diplomatic relations between Mauritania and Senegal, which were broken off during the deportations in April 1989, would be re-established three years later in April 1992 without resolving the issue of the refugees. The government of Senegal, like that of Mauritania, apparently succumbed to pressure from France to re-establish relations in the interests of diffusing the tensions along the border and reinstating the previous uneasy peace.

The refugees have never received full refugee status in Senegal due to a provision of Senegalese law that prohibits the recognition of an entire group as refugees. Refugee status must be granted individually, through a National Eligibility Commission. A case-by-case review of the thousands of refugees currently living in Senegal would be impossible to conduct; accordingly, the Mauritanians are not recognized as *bona fide* refugees by either the Mauritanian or the Senegalese authorities.

The official Senegalese policy is to ensure that the refugees return to Mauritania with the assistance of the Mauritanian government. Senegalese officials claim that the return of the refugees was part and parcel of their discussions with the Mauritanians when relations between the two countries were re-established, and that the issues continues to be discussed, even though no apparent progress has been made. A high-ranking Senegalese official said that even though he doubted that black's rights would ever be respected in Mauritania, "one way or another, the refugees will go back. Even if all their [the refugees] conditions are not met."[29]

According to a survey conducted in January-February 1993 by the United Nations High Commissioner for Refugees (UNHCR), a clear majority of the refugees want to return to Mauritania.[30] Also in early 1993, the United

---

[28]Interview in the Department of Bakel, Senegal, February 27, 1991.

[29]Interview in Dakar, Senegal, November 5, 1993.

[30]Interviews with UNHCR officials in Dakar and St. Louis, Senegal, October-November 1993. The survey was conducted between January 26 and February 16, 1993. The results were as follows: in the Department of Dagana, 74 percent wanted to go back

Nations' World Food Program (WFP) began progressively reducing the food rations for the refugees, thereby increasing the pressure on them to return.[31]

Some refugees have gone back: In 1992 and 1993, the UNHCR registered 1,400 refugees who returned.[32] Thus far, none of the cases constitutes a model for repatriation. A group of villagers from Dabaye, for instance, returned due to the intervention of the family of a *marabout*, a religious leader, named Cheik Sidiya in Mauritania. They went back without any guarantees concerning the restoration of their lands or their rights. Reports indicate that they are now farming some land that belongs to the marabout, but have not been able to recover rights to their own land.

Human Rights Watch/Africa's discussions with individual refugees reveal that they want to go back only under certain conditions: the return of or compensation for their belongings, jobs, and lands; the restoration of their civil rights, including their citizenship; and UNHCR responsibility for their repatriation. Unless there is an end to human rights abuses against the blacks in Mauritania, refugees will continue to flee to neighboring countries. In addition, until the legitimate rights of the refugees are addressed, they will continue to constitute an ongoing source of tension and instability in the region.

---

to Mauritania, 25 percent wanted to stay in Senegal, and 1 percent had no opinion; in the Department of Podor, 93 percent wanted to go back, 5 percent wanted to stay, 2 percent had no opinion; in the Department of Matam, 51 percent wanted to go back, 47 percent wanted to stay, 2 percent had no opinion; in the Department of Bakel, 52 percent wanted to go back, 47 percent wanted to stay, and 1 percent had no opinion.

[31]The World Food Program is reducing rations because it considers the emergency phase to be ending, to be replaced by the local installation phase. From February-June 1993, rations were reduced by five percent; from June-December 1993, they were reduced by ten percent more.

[32]According to the UNHCR in Dakar, the refugees left in two main waves: on September 29, 1992 from the Department of Matam, and on August 2, 1993, 705 went back from three villages in the Department of Podor -- Dabaye, Toulny Diamy and Mdioundou.

11
THE INTERNATIONAL RESPONSE

The international community has effectively ignored the severe human rights abuses reported above, and the Mauritanian authorities have benefited from the country's international obscurity to systematically marginalize and persecute its black population. In fact, only when these violations reached huge proportions -- such as the forcible expulsion of thousands of blacks in 1989 and the massacre of at least 500 blacks in 1991 -- has there been any significant echo in the international arena. This silence is due, in part, to the lack of geopolitical interests for the Western powers, as well as to the Organization of African Unity's (OAU) policy of noninterference in the internal affairs of member states.

The events of 1989 between Mauritania and Senegal did draw a number of foreign governments and international organizations into mediation efforts between Senegal and Mauritania. These included the OAU, which got involved at the outset of the crisis, as well as the European Community (now the European Union, or EU), which appointed a former Belgian prime minister, Leo Tindemans, as mediator in October 1990. However, the focus was almost exclusively on the international aspects of the dispute. The mediating parties avoided actions that would alienate the Mauritanian government, such as public statements about its human rights record. Since the government's treatment of the black population constituted the core of the conflict between the two countries, the international community missed an important opportunity to bring these abuses under public scrutiny -- an important first step toward ending them.

U.S. POLICY

The U.S. has few political or economic interests in Mauritania, especially after the latter's support for Iraq in the Gulf War, and has openly criticized Mauritania on human rights grounds. In 1991, the U.S. ended all bilateral assistance and authorized the U.S. ambassador to make private *démarches* about human rights concerns.

The cut off of U.S. aid came in February 1991, as information began to surface about the deaths of hundreds of black political prisoners. The United States suspended the last of its bilateral aid to Mauritania — $125,000 for International Military and Education Training (IMET). State Department sources reported to Human Rights Watch/Africa that the U.S. Embassy had told the Mauritanian government that the aid was cut because of human rights violations, including the deaths in detention, but no public confirmation of this reason was ever issued.

The decision to cutoff all U.S. assistance sent a strong signal to the Mauritanian authorities. However, U.S. aid had been relatively small: in fiscal year 1990, U.S. aid to Mauritania was approximately $6 million. This included $590,000 in development assistance, some $5 million in food aid, and $124,000 in military training.

The Bush administration did issue a strong public condemnation of Mauritanian abuses during hearings on the Maghreb held on June 19, 1991, before the House Subcommittees on African Affairs and on Human Rights and International Organizations. Testifying for the administration, James Bishop, senior deputy assistant secretary of state for human rights and humanitarian affairs, condemned "repeated human rights abuses consisting primarily of discrimination by the Maur [Moor] dominated government against non-Maur ethnic groups." He described the detention and brutal treatment of the alleged coup plotters, and the murder of 500 to 600 of them. He continued:

> Beginning in November 1990, our human rights concerns in Mauritania focused increasingly on the arbitrary arrest, incommunicado detention and brutal treatment of an estimated 2,000 to 3,000 black Mauritanians for alleged participation in a conspiracy to overthrow the government. These individuals were drawn primarily from the Halpulaar ethnic group, the same group which suffered mass expulsions in 1989 and in early 1990...We repeatedly urged the Government to grant these detainees due process promptly or to release them. To our knowledge, none of the detainees was charged or brought to trial.

Ambassador Bishop also welcomed the Mauritanian government's pledge to democratize, but noted a number of government actions which contradicted that pledge, such as the beating of peaceful demonstrators and the arrest of democracy activists.

In November 1991, the Bush administration took steps against Mauritania at the World Bank. Citing human rights violations, the U.S. changed its voting position on multilateral development bank loans to Mauritania. The Treasury Department instructed the U.S. executive director at the World Bank to abstain on World Bank loans to Mauritania, except those involving basic human needs.[1] Mauritania thus joined China, Equatorial Guinea, Iran, and Sudan as the only countries for which the U.S. has adopted this policy at the World Bank on human rights grounds.[2]

The U.S. Congress has also expressed its concern about human rights abuses in Mauritania. In July 1991, a "sense of congress" resolution was passed which condemned human rights abuses against black ethnic groups in Mauritania and called on the Mauritanian government to appoint an independent commission to investigate the deaths in detention.

In February 1992, a high-ranking official of the State Department visited Nouakchott and delivered a strong message to President Taya concerning ongoing human rights violations against the black population. Sources in the State Department indicated that the U.S. official made it clear that improvement in the human rights performance of the Mauritanian government was the key to any amelioration of U.S. - Mauritanian relations.

The Clinton administration continued to take a strong position against Mauritania, and in June 1993 U.S. Trade Representative Michael Kantor announced the suspension of Mauritania's special trade benefits under the Generalized System of Preferences (GSP). Under the GSP, developing countries can export selected goods duty-free to the U.S., but such benefits can be suspended if a government is found to systematically violate worker rights. In the case of Mauritania, the abuse involved the ongoing practice of slavery.

---

[1]Section 701 (a) of Title VII of Public Law 95-118, as amended, states: "The United States Government, in connection with its voice and vote in the International Bank for Reconstruction and Development, the International Development Association, the International Finance Corporation, the Inter-American Development Bank, the African Development Fund, the Asian Development Bank, and the African Development Bank, shall advance the cause of human rights, including by seeking to channel assistance toward countries other than those whose governments engage in --

> (1) a pattern of gross violations of internationally recognized human rights, such as torture or cruel, inhumane or degrading treatment or punishment, prolonged detention without charges, or other flagrant denial of life, liberty and the security of person...

[2]In addition, the U.S. is required to oppose loans, grants, and credits to countries on the State Department designated terrorist list -- Cuba, Iran, Iraq, Libya, North Korea, Syria, and Sudan -- and to drug producing or major drug-transit countries -- Burma, Iran, and Syria.

FRENCH POLICY

France, as the former colonial power and Mauritania's principal source of foreign aid, has more influence in Mauritania than any other Western country. The prominence of the French role in Mauritania has been particularly enhanced since the Gulf War, because financial assistance from the Gulf states was cut off after Mauritania supported Iraq.

French bilateral aid to Mauritania in 1990 was approximately 300 million francs (roughly $52 million), which included food aid and some 250 technical advisors in the fields of agriculture, health and education. France also provided a smaller amount of technical military cooperation to Mauritania. Although the aid figures for subsequent years are not available, sources in the French government have confirmed that the aid in 1991 and 1992 was at least the same as 1990 and probably higher. France is Mauritania's principal trading partner, providing 40 percent of its imports and absorbing 11 percent of its exports.

The French government relies almost entirely on quiet diplomacy to pressure the Mauritanian authorities and does not make public statements about human rights abuses. According to sources in the French government, France believes that it has a greater responsibility to preserve peace between states than to get involved in the internal affairs of those states. By maintaining friendly relations with the Mauritanian government, the French contend that they can exert more effective influence on human rights matters.

The French government maintains that Mauritania should be rewarded for its democratic progress. While its democratic institutions may not be perfect, French officials argue that the Taya regime has made significant improvements. An official of the French Embassy in Dakar summarized the French position as follows: "There has been a certain amelioration in the past couple of years. Democracy doesn't take root in five years, ten years, even fifty years. But Mauritania is on the right road."[3]

In geopolitical terms, the French consider Mauritania part of both the Maghreb and black Africa. Since France has important interests in the Maghreb countries, it is careful not to offend those countries by criticizing the Arabization policies of the Mauritanian authorities.

It is clear that when the French government seeks to pressure the Mauritanian authorities on human rights grounds, its actions have significant resonance. For example, the releases of political prisoners in March 1991 and the announcement of reforms in April 1991 were due in large part to French

---

[3]Interview with Bertrand Rault, Premier Conseiller at the French Embassy in Dakar, Senegal, November 5, 1993.

pressure. The March 1991 amnesty was declared just after a trip to Nouakchott by Michel Vauzelle, president of the Foreign Affairs Committee of the French National Assembly. President Taya's April 1991 speech on democratization was made several days after Roland Dumas, then foreign minister, visited Mauritania. Dumas's visit also prompted the Mauritanian government's promise of parliamentary elections and its appointment of an internal commission of inquiry into the massacre of 1990–91. The French officials, however, made no public statements during these visits, nor have they at any time publicly called for an independent commission of inquiry into human rights abuses.[4]

In early 1993, an incident occurred which threw France's relations with Mauritania into stark relief: Mauritanian Col. Sid'Ahmed Ould Boïlil, one of the principal architects of the massacre of 1990-91, was admitted to France to attend training workshops at the École de Guerre. Mauritanian exiles and human rights activists in both France and Mauritania launched a campaign to force the French government to live up to its obligations under the Convention Against Torture and Other Cruel, Inhuman or Degrading Treatment, to which France is a signatory, and take measures against the colonel, including taking him into custody.[5] Ultimately, Ould Boïlil was recalled by his government and, with French approval, returned to Mauritania. Needless to say, Ould Boïlil did not face prosecution or investigation of any kind upon his return.

The most striking illustration of France's refusal to publicly add human rights to its dealings with the Mauritanian government came in mid-December 1993, when President Taya conducted his first official visit to Paris. From December 13–15, Taya was received by Prime Minister Edouard Balladur, the presidents of both the National Assembly and the Senate, and even President

---

[4]A delegation from the National Assembly went to Nouakchott during the presidential elections in January 1992. They issued a statement which praised the free atmosphere during the election campaign, but expressed serious reservations about technical irregularities during the actual voting which prevented large numbers of people from voting. They also condemned the violent incidents in Nouakchott and Nouadhibou after the elections.

[5]Article 6, paragraph 1 of the Convention states: "...any State Party in whose territory a person alleged to have committed any offense referred to in article 4 [acts of torture] is present shall take him into custody or take other legal measures to ensure his presence. The custody and other legal measures shall be as provided in the law of that State but may be continued only for such time as is necessary to enable any criminal or extradition proceedings to be instituted."

François Mitterand. According to the a spokesperson for the Ministry of Foreign Affairs, Richard Duqué, France congratulated Taya on his country's "progress in the rule of law since the January 1992 elections."[6] Commenting on Taya's visit, the usually pro-Mauritanian French journal *Jeune Afrique* noted: "Under these conditions, it was hardly surprising that none of Maaouya Ould Taya's interlocutors spoke to him about human rights or democracy: they must have found the results in these areas generally satisfying."[7]

THE WORLD BANK

The World Bank is a principal lender to Mauritania, and therefore wields considerable influence. Over five years, from 1993 to 1997, the Bank will be spending $90 million in Mauritania, all of which is International Development Association (IDA) assistance.[8] Mauritania is not eligible for regular Bank loans from the International Bank for Reconstruction and Development (IBRD), because it is considered too poor to repay the loans.

Human rights conditionality as such is contrary to the bank policies, since the bank's articles of agreement prohibit it from taking into account anything but "economic considerations." However, the bank is increasingly experimenting with "non-economic" factors, including analyzing governance issues. Ever since the World Bank published its 1989 study titled *Sub-Saharan Africa: From Crisis to Sustainable Growth*, there has been a growing recognition of the need to improve "governance" in Africa if sustainable development is to be achieved. The study states:

> It is not just the unpredictability of policies that discourages investment [in Africa], but also the uncertainty about their interpretation and application by officials. This problem is exacerbated by the frequent lack of a reliable legal framework to enforce contracts. The rule of law needs to be established. In many instances this implies rehabilitation of the judicial system,

---

[6]"Arrivée à Paris du président," *Agence France-Presse*, December 14, 1993.

[7]François Soudan, "Mauritanie: Le bon élève, "*Jeune Afrique*, December 23, 1993-January 5, 1994.

[8]IDA assistance is geared toward the poorest countries, considered to be those with an annual per capita GNP of $610 or less. IDA loans must be repaid, but without interest and with such a long grace period that they are considered to be virtually grant aid.

> independence of the judiciary, scrupulous respect for the law and human rights at every level of government, transparent accounting of public monies, and independent public auditors responsible to a representative legislature, not to an executive. Independent institutions are necessary to ensure public accountability.[9]

Bank programs have continued in Mauritania, despite rampant human rights abuses and a lack of the rule of law. For example, the bank negotiated an agricultural sectoral adjustment loan with the Mauritanian government in 1990, a key component of which is devoted to land reform. The issue of land reform is linked to the government's cynical land policies throughout the 1980s, but especially the blatantly discriminatory expropriation of traditional black lands during and after the expulsions of 1989–1990. Accordingly, the situation of the refugees in Senegal and their demands to return to their lands should impact the bank's program. Unfortunately, the bank is not publicly raising the issue of the refugees, which has given rise to fears that the bank's programs will effectively legalize the expropriation of black lands along the Senegal River Valley, rather than instituting a more equitable application of the principles of land reform.

Based on the Bank's policies concerning promoting "good governance" as well as protecting traditional land tenure and indigenous peoples' rights, it is imperative that the Bank bring pressure to bear on the Mauritanian government on human rights grounds.

THE EUROPEAN UNION AND THE EUROPEAN PARLIAMENT

European Union

Mauritania receives considerable aid from the EU and the aid is allocated over a five-year period in accordance with the Lomé Conventions.[10] Under the Lome IV Convention, which covers 1990 to 1995, the EU will provide 61 million ECU[11] (approximately $68.26 million) under the National Indicative

---

[9]The World Bank, *Sub-Saharan Africa: From Crisis to Sustainable Growth*, Washington D.C., 1989, p. 192.

[10]The Lome IV Convention is a cooperation agreement, signed in December 1989, involving the 68 African, Caribbean and Pacific States (ACP) and the 12 member states of the European Community.

[11]ECU stands for European Currency Unit.

Program for infrastructure development and rural development, 18 million ECU ($20.14 million) for structural adjustment, and approximately 14 million ECU ($15.67 million) for stabilization of export earnings. In addition, the European Investment Bank will provide 11 million ECU ($13.97 million) in credits over the same five-year period, although these credits must be repaid.

While the EU rarely suspends its aid on human rights grounds, there are numerous mechanisms for leverage. In cases of serious human rights violations, the EU can take a series of actions, beginning with a private démarche to the government, followed by a public statement, and finally, suspension of aid. In Africa, aid has been suspended on human rights grounds in the following countries: Sudan and Zaire, in late 1990 and January 1992, respectively, and in Malawi in 1992 (it was reinstated in 1993).[12]

For the first time, however, the Lomé IV agreement contains human rights language. Chapter 1, Article 5 of the convention states:

> 1. Cooperation shall be directed toward development centered on man, the main protagonist and beneficiary of development, which thus entails respect for and promotion of human rights. Cooperation operations shall thus be conceived in accordance with the positive approach, where respect for human rights is recognized as a basic factor of real development and where cooperation is conceived as a contribution to the promotion of these rights.
>
> In this context, development policy and cooperation are closely linked with the respect for and enjoyment of fundamental human rights....

The specific agreement between the EU and the Mauritanian government, signed in Nouakchott on April 18, 1991, also refers to "the respect and promotion of all human rights" (Section 7 of Chapter I) as a necessary component of development.

Nevertheless, there has been little concrete action by the EU regarding human rights in Mauritania. One of the only public statements was made on April 29, 1990, when a press release was issued about the continuing dispute between Senegal and Mauritania, calling on the two parties to "engage in negotiations in order to resolve their dispute." It made no mention of the myriad

---

[12]In addition, the EU has had no cooperation with Somalia or Liberia since the EU delegations were evacuated under emergency situations. For both countries, it is the lack of a state that is cited as the reason for no cooperation.

violations of human rights that had accompanied the conflict.

European Parliament

The European Parliament has commented publicly on human rights. On May 25, 1989, the European Parliament issued a resolution expressing concern about the ethnic conflict between Senegal and Mauritania, citing:

> the loss of countless human lives among the Mauritanian and Senegalese populations, the destruction of property, the forced repatriation of thousands of people to their respective countries and the deterioration of relations between the two neighboring states.

However, the resolution did little more than call on the member states to determine the EU's position and ask the European Commission to provide humanitarian aid to the families of the victims and the refugees in both countries.

On April 18, 1991, the parliament issued a resolution focusing on the serious human rights violations in Mauritania. It stated:

> The European Parliament is deeply concerned about recent testimonies which followed the release of certain prisoners, and about the serious and numerous violations of human rights perpetrated in Mauritania. These violations are believed to have led to the execution without trial, or the torture to death, of at least 200 political prisoners; and to the mistreatment inflicted on hundreds of people who were detained without trial under cruel conditions.

The resolution went on to condemn "the racist nature of the persecution, since all the victims were blacks," and called for an independent investigation into these executions and other human rights violations in Mauritania, and the prosecution of those responsible.

ORGANIZATION OF AFRICAN UNITY (OAU)

The OAU formed a subcommittee to engage in mediation efforts between the Senegal and Mauritania after the events of 1989. The subcommittee took a number of initiatives, including sending fact-finding missions to Dakar and Nouakchott and organizing contacts between the two countries in Paris and Cairo.

The subcommittee focused only on the international aspects of the conflict, such as reestablishing diplomatic relations, resuming postal and telecommunication links, reestablishing air links and assuring security in the border area. Attention was not paid to the human rights aspects of the conflict, nor were any statements made suggesting that human rights violations were relevant to the negotiations.

12
RECOMMENDATIONS

To the Government of Mauritania:

- Acknowledge the expulsion of the black Mauritanians into Senegal and Mali, and permit them to return to Mauritania under conditions of security and dignity, including the return of or compensation for their land, belongings, and employment;
- Repeal the June 1993 amnesty, and launch an independent investigation of those responsible for gross abuses of human rights, notably the deportations of 1989-90 and the massacre of 1990-91, and bring to justice those responsible;
- End the military occupation of the Senegal River Valley, and take immediate steps to introduce the rule of law;
- End the practice of slavery, and prosecute slaveowners who refuse to comply with the law;
- Permit all blacks in Mauritania to move freely in the country, without fear of arbitrary arrest or harassment;
- Allow independent human rights groups to operate in Mauritania and recognize their legal status, and give access to international human rights organizations that seek to conduct fact-finding investigations.

To the International Community:

- Publicly raise the issue of human rights abuses against the blacks in Mauritania;
- Oppose loans to the government of Mauritania, except those addressing basic human needs, until the refugees are permitted to return and receive equitable compensation and an independent inquiry is conducted into human rights abuses.
- For those loans that are already negotiated, such as the agricultural structural adjustment loan of the World Bank, undertake special efforts to ensure that the refugees whose land was expropriated in a discriminatory manner by the Mauritanian authorities are able to participate in the revised land tenure system.
- Ensure that the United Nations agencies - United Nations High Commission on Refugees and World Food Program - continue to support the refugees in Senegal and Mali until they are able to return home with guarantees of security.